jQuery Mobile First Look

Discover the endless possibilities offered by jQuery
Mobile for rapid mobile web development

Giulio Bai

BIRMINGHAM - MUMBAI

jQuery Mobile First Look

First published: June 2011

Production Reference: 1170611

Published by Packt Publishing Ltd.
32 Lincoln Road
Olton
Birmingham, B27 6PA, UK.

ISBN 978-1-849515-90-0

www.packtpub.com

Cover Image by Asher Wishkerman (a.wishkerman@mpic.de)

Credits

Author
Giulio Bai

Reviewers
Raymond Camden
Matthew Makai
Silas Jesufemi Olatayo
Federico M. Rinaldi

Development Editor
Meeta Rajani

Technical Editors
Gauri Iyer
Manasi Poonthottam

Copy Editor
Leonard D'silva

Project Coordinator
Michelle Quadros

Proofreader
Aaron Nash

Indexer
Tejal Daruwale

Graphics
Nilesh R. Mohite

Production Coordinator
Adline Swetha Jesuthas

Cover Work
Adline Swetha Jesuthas

About the Author

Giulio Bai is a law student living in Italy who spends most of his time toying with stuff which doesn't have anything to do with law.

Even after trying to keep the list of his past achievements as short as possible, the number of projects he joined in (and invariably sunk short thereafter) makes it hard to narrow down his interests to programming and carousels alone.

It should be made clear that any claim of responsibility for those unfortunate ventures is wholeheartedly rejected – they never had the necessary potential to make it anyway.

This incredibly interesting and valuable bunch of paper sheets (or bits, if you're reading an e-book) has been made available to you – my fellow readers – thanks to the jQuery community, who have decided to start developing something new I could write about. Cheers to them!

About the Reviewers

Raymond Camden is a software architect for FirstComp focusing on ColdFusion and RIA development. A long time ColdFusion user, Raymond has worked on numerous ColdFusion books including the ColdFusion Web Application Construction Kit and has contributed to the Fusion Authority Quarterly Update, and the ColdFusion Developers Journal. He also presents at conferences and contributes to online webzines. He founded many community web sites including jQueryBloggers.com, CFLib.org, ColdFusionPortal.org, and is the author of open source applications, including the popular BlogCFC (`www.blogcfc.com`) blogging application. Raymond is an Adobe Community Professional. He is the happily married proud father of three kids and is somewhat of a Star Wars nut. Raymond can be reached at his blog (`www.coldfusionjedi.com`) or via e-mail at `ray@camdenfamily.com`.

Matthew Makai is a technology consultant specializing in data exploration, analysis, and visualization with Excella Consulting in Arlington, Virginia. He is particularly interested in enhancing personal and business decisions with mobile web applications and data visualization. Matthew earned his Computer Science B.S. at James Madison University, his Computer Science M.S. at Virginia Tech, and his Management of Information Technology M.S. at the University of Virginia.

Matthew writes about big data trends and solutions to technical problems with Hadoop, Google Web Toolkit, JQuery Mobile, and NoSQL-related technologies at `http://mmakai.com/`.

www.PacktPub.com

Support files, eBooks, discount offers and more

You might want to visit www.PacktPub.com for support files and downloads related to your book.

Did you know that Packt offers eBook versions of every book published, with PDF and ePub files available? You can upgrade to the eBook version at www.PacktPub.com and as a print book customer, you are entitled to a discount on the eBook copy. Get in touch with us at service@packtpub.com for more details.

At www.PacktPub.com, you can also read a collection of free technical articles, sign up for a range of free newsletters and receive exclusive discounts and offers on Packt books and eBooks.

http://PacktLib.PacktPub.com

Do you need instant solutions to your IT questions? PacktLib is Packt's online digital book library. Here, you can access, read and search across Packt's entire library of books.

Why Subscribe?

- Fully searchable across every book published by Packt
- Copy and paste, print and bookmark content
- On demand and accessible via web browser

Free Access for Packt account holders

If you have an account with Packt at www.PacktPub.com, you can use this to access PacktLib today and view nine entirely free books. Simply use your login credentials for immediate access.

Table of Contents

Preface

The jQuery Mobile framework is jQuery's latest rabbit out of the hat project. The jQuery Mobile framework is open source and is supported by all the big players: iOS, Android, Bada, BlackBerry, Nokia, Adobe, and so, covering all the names behind the project. It is a truly cross platform framework and porting applications made in jQuery mobile will be a snap with this new technology in your hands. Get to grips with everything you need to know to sprint through developing high end web applications for mobiles.

jQuery Mobile First Look will show you the features of the jQuery Mobile framework, what they do, and how they can be used. It covers the installation thoroughly on all the machines, as it is found with any new technology that the most difficult part is getting people to correctly install the product.

From installation to specifications and from designing to deployment this book covers all the factors that you need to know before starting your own mobile web application development. Starting with an introduction to jQuery Mobile, the book will give you an overview of the key features of the framework and how they can be used to implement a mobile web application. Development tips and troubleshooting add to the standard information contained in these pages. The topics covered include everything the jQuery Mobile developer needs to know in order to create a full-feature web application for mobile devices. Ranging from a comparison of jQuery mobile with other popular frameworks and its installation on various Operating Systems to theming pages, website layout, and content formatting, the book presents information about buttons, toolbars, dialogs, forms, and list views, as well as suggesting best practices and workarounds to accomplish things in an alternative way.

jQuery Mobile First Look will help you learn one of the most promising JavaScript mobile frameworks and grasp how widgets and elements work and what you can do to customize and enhance their behavior.

A by-example guide that will let you explore all the features of jQuery Mobile and get you ready for all the mobile web development you will do.

What this book covers

Chapter 1, What is jQuery Mobile?: We will give some background information about the jQuery Mobile framework but, most important of all, will discuss the differences between the various mobile frameworks out there and explain why jQuery Mobile outperforms its competitor. Installation and other miscellaneous information are also included.

Chapter 2, Organizing Content: Pages and Dialogs: We'll see how pages are structured in jQuery Mobile and how can we link between them or create multi-page templates. In a very similar fashion, dialogs will also be discussed.

Chapter 3, Configuring and Extending jQuery Mobile: As the name suggests, we'll learn how to configure the default settings, handle events (taping, swiping, animations, and so on), and take advantage of jQuery Mobile's built-in methods and utilities to further interact with the elements on our web page.

Chapter 4, Reading, Writing, Communicating: Content: This chapter addresses the issue of content, explaining how it will be displayed by default and what we can do to change the way it looks. Usage of elements such as grids (to organize information) and collapsible blocks (for hiding and showing paragraphs) will be revealed.

Chapter 5, Navigation Made Easier: Toolbars: The importance of toolbars in jQuery Mobile needs to be pointed out; and in this chapter we'll understand how to use toolbars to provide additional options and control to the user, and how to position, theme, and enhance them in every possible way.

Chapter 6, Mobile Clicking: Buttons: Buttons and their key role in mobile development: how they can be grouped, displayed customized for a better user experience in a mobile enviroinment.

Chapter 7, Transmitting Information: Forms: This chapter deals with creating forms and submitting data via AJAX using jQuery Mobile. We'll also have a look at how to implement sliders, toggle switches, search inputs into our fieldset elements.

Chapter 8, Organizing Information. List Views: We don't want to miss out on list views, which play a huge role in jQuery Mobile when it comes to organizing and laying out our content. This chapter presents the basics of list elements and guides you through the realization of a music player interface.

Appendix A, API Calls and Properties: This appendix presents a list of the API calls and properties to interact with jQuery Mobile internals.

Appendix B, Resources and Troubleshooting: This appendix presents a list of useful resources, development tools, and troubleshooting in order to better understand how jQuery (Mobile) and JavaScript work together.

What you need for this book

In order to get the best out of this book, you only need a web browser and a copy of jQuery Mobile – we'll discuss how to actually grab one in *Chapter 1 , What is jQuery Mobile?*.

It's also suggested to use Firefox as a web browser in conjunction with the firebug extension; alternatively, any other browser with their respective developer plugin is on par (see *Appendix B, Resources and Troubleshooting* to learn how to install and enable such plugins).

Who this book is for

This is a First Look book that allows existing jQuery users to get a look at the features of jQuery mobile. It is targeted at jQuery users who want to enter the exciting world of mobile web development. All you need is the basics of jQuery and an interest to get involved with mobile development and you can use this book as a launch-pad for your future ventures in mobile web development with jQuery Mobile framework.

Conventions

In this book, you will find a number of styles of text that distinguish between different kinds of information. Here are some examples of these styles, and an explanation of their meaning.

Code words in text are shown as follows: "We then wrap all of it into a container which has a `data-role="fieldcontain"` attribute".

A block of code is set as follows:

```
[<title>jQuery Mobile Page Structure Test</title>
<link rel="stylesheet" href="jquery.mobile-latest.min.css"" />
<script src="jquery-latest.min.js"></script>
<script src="jquery.mobile-latest.min.js"></script>
```

When we wish to draw your attention to a particular part of a code block, the relevant lines or items are set in bold:

```
<script src="jquery.js"></script>
```

```
<script src="custom-scripting.js"></script>
<script src="jquery-mobile.js"></script>
```

New terms and **important words** are shown in bold. Words that you see on the screen, in menus or dialog boxes for example, appear in the text like this: "The **Cancel** button should be included this time, as there is no **Close** button in the top-left corner".

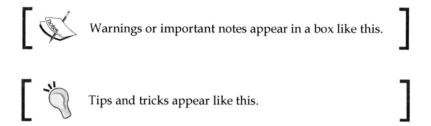

Warnings or important notes appear in a box like this.

Tips and tricks appear like this.

Reader feedback

Feedback from our readers is always welcome. Let us know what you think about this book—what you liked or may have disliked. Reader feedback is important for us to develop titles that you really get the most out of.

To send us general feedback, simply send an e-mail to feedback@packtpub.com, and mention the book title via the subject of your message.

If there is a book that you need and would like to see us publish, please send us a note in the **SUGGEST A TITLE** form on www.packtpub.com or e-mail suggest@packtpub.com.

If there is a topic that you have expertise in and you are interested in either writing or contributing to a book, see our author guide on www.packtpub.com/authors.

Customer support

Now that you are the proud owner of a Packt book, we have a number of things to help you to get the most from your purchase.

Downloading the example code

You can download the example code files for all Packt books you have purchased from your account at http://www.PacktPub.com. If you purchased this book elsewhere, you can visit http://www.PacktPub.com/support and register to have the files e-mailed directly to you.

Errata

Although we have taken every care to ensure the accuracy of our content, mistakes do happen. If you find a mistake in one of our books—maybe a mistake in the text or the code—we would be grateful if you would report this to us. By doing so, you can save other readers from frustration and help us improve subsequent versions of this book. If you find any errata, please report them by visiting http://www.packtpub.com/support, selecting your book, clicking on the **errata submission form** link, and entering the details of your errata. Once your errata are verified, your submission will be accepted and the errata will be uploaded on our website, or added to any list of existing errata, under the Errata section of that title. Any existing errata can be viewed by selecting your title from http://www.packtpub.com/support.

Piracy

Piracy of copyright material on the Internet is an ongoing problem across all media. At Packt, we take the protection of our copyright and licenses very seriously. If you come across any illegal copies of our works, in any form, on the Internet, please provide us with the location address or website name immediately so that we can pursue a remedy.

Please contact us at copyright@packtpub.com with a link to the suspected pirated material.

We appreciate your help in protecting our authors, and our ability to bring you valuable content.

Questions

You can contact us at questions@packtpub.com if you are having a problem with any aspect of the book, and we will do our best to address it.

1
What is jQuery Mobile?

The first time I heard (well, read) about jQuery Mobile, I was lying on a beach. I lazily reached out to my Palm Smartphone – being careful not to spill a drop of the juicy drink I was sipping onto my beloved device – and connected to the Internet to check the latest news.

The fact that jQuery was undergoing a process of consistent improvement in order to make it work smoothly will surely trigger your curiosity as it triggered mine. In this chapter, we're going to approach the jQuery Mobile framework for the very first time, and understand how the whole thing works and can be implemented in our own web applications.

Using jQuery Mobile, we will be able to develop mobile solutions that work smoothly on the majority of mobile OS: the new-born library already supports Android, Blackberry OS6, Fennec (by Mozilla), HP WebOS (Palm handhelds), iOS (thus iPhone, iPod Touch, iPad), and Opera Mobile. Additionally, the roadmap includes, amongst others, MeeGo, Windows Mobile, and Symbian as platforms which are going to be supported in the near future.

In this chapter, we shall understand:

- How jQuery Mobile was born
- jQuery Mobile and other libraries
- Why choose jQuery Mobile?
- How to get jQuery Mobile
- jQuery Mobile in action
- Getting involved

How jQuery Mobile was born

jQuery Mobile was first announced as an independent project on August 11, 2010, and described on the jQuery blog as the work that we've been doing to bring jQuery to mobile devices. Not only is the core jQuery library being improved to work across all of the major mobile platforms, but we're also working to release a complete, unified, mobile UI framework.

The jQuery Project developers worked hard (and are still working hard) on making jQuery Core work well against the major web browsers, and bug fixes and improvements are released periodically in order to make sure that standards are kept high.

The jQuery Mobile project has caught on to the promising augment of mobile sites and interest in the mobile technology, and is now trying to extend its reach of jQuery to help build applications capable of running along with the so-called "desktop" Web.

jQuery mobile and other libraries

Before getting involved and learning about jQuery Mobile, a legitimate question to ask would concern the comparison with other more or less established and used JavaScript libraries, which claim to have the same goals.

For example, how good is jQuery Mobile compared to any of the following?

- jQTouch
- Sencha Touch
- iUI
- iWebKit

Let's find out!

jQTouch

While jQuery Mobile is a relatively recent entry in the mobile world, jQTouch dates back to 2009, when David Kaneda created an open source jQuery plugin for mobile development on the iPhone.

Due to its close relationship (and dependency) with jQuery, the plugin files themselves are quite heavy.

Although aware of the problem, jQTouch developers decided not to remove the dependency from the jQuery core.

Some people have said they'd like to see the jQuery dependency removed from jQTouch to decrease the download size. The reasoning is that jQuery has a lot of code dedicated to legacy desktop browsers (that is, older, discontinued versions), and is therefore dead-weight on mobile devices.

Who is it for?

The jQTouch development team has decided to keep the project strictly focused on WebKit-enabled devices (that is, iPhone, iPod Touch, Palm WebOS, and Android), all of which have a relatively small screen. It provides native animations, automatic navigation, and a customizable theming system for WebKit browsers.

According to their blog, we understand that, even though jQTouch runs fine on larger-screen devices, it's not its intended use, and therefore the UI will not take advantage of the additional space.

Applications developed with jQTouch will certainly run fine on iPads and other tablet devices, but we aren't going to automatically convert to a more tablet-friendly UI that takes advantage of the additional real estate.

Because of the type of plugin and its overall structure, jQTouch is a package geared primarily towards web designers and novice web-application developers. jQTouch developers themselves recommend more expert software programmers to use their other standalone project Sencha Touch.

How does it look?

A sample image that shows jQTouch's look and feel is shown in the following screenshot representing the user interface of the clock demo. It can be found at the jQTouch website (`http://jqtouch.com`).

As it's easily noticeable, jQTouch shows some kind of consistency with other UI that resemble a native-like iPhone application.

What should I remember?

A few key things to remember about jQTouch are:

- It is easy to set up.
- Native WebKit animations. But only WebKit (no support for other platforms.)
- Theming system.
- Small screen devices only.

Sencha Touch

Shortly after the release of his jQTouch, David Kaneda decided to release a completely different package, with more or less the same goals, but not dependent on jQuery anymore.

Sencha Touch was born, and it is still seen as an alternative to jQTouch when speaking of tablets and other devices of the same kind. The interesting thing about this is the complete separation of the two projects; one (jQTouch) is a plugin for jQuery, and depends on the popular library, while the other (Sencha Touch) is a framework and provides a number of functionalities the former could not develop (that is, API).

Being developed as a standalone framework, Sencha Touch is also more lightweight than its sister project, JQTouch, which needs the whole jQuery framework to work correctly.

Who is it for?

Even being an alternative for jQTouch, Sencha Touch targets the same set of devices, but adds support for tablets:

> *If you are in need of a JavaScript library that magically updates your UI for everything from small screens, to tablets, to desktops, check out Sencha Touch.*

Sencha Touch offers a pure JavaScript API for building powerful applications which, ideally, are developed by software and mobile developers looking forward to create a product with advanced layouts, functionality, and interfaces.

How does it look?

Sencha Touch looks simple, but refined. Its graphical user interface is very similar to the native UI of the devices on which the library runs, in order to create a feeling of consistency with the original interface.

This is how the buttons appear:

What should I remember?

Sencha Touch stands out because of the following:

- Lighter than most other frameworks
- Unfortunately, still looks good on WebKit devices only

- Works great on tablets
- JavaScript API

iUI

First and foremost, let's get this one right; iUI is not a JavaScript library. Not in the traditional way, at least.

The iUI project (as we know it today) is actually the outcome of a simple hack by Joe Hewitt to create iPhone applications, called iphonenav; we can modify its behavior and default configuration by changing the markup. No JavaScript scripting is generally needed.

Going directly to the introductory post by the author himself, iUI is explained as follows:

Its goal is simply to turn ordinary standards-based HTML into a polished, usable interface that meets the high standards set by Apple's own native iPhone apps. As much as possible, iUI maps common HTML idioms to iPhone interface conventions. For example, the `<ul>` and `<li>` tags are used to create hierarchical side-scrolling navigation. Ordinary `<a>` links load with a sliding animation while keeping you on the original page instead of loading an entirely new one. A simple set of CSS classes can be used to designate things like modal dialogs, preference panels, and on/off switches.

iUI is now maintained in Google Code, and aims at making mobile developers feel like HTML is the native UI language for the iPhone, as there is no need to write any JavaScript code to see the magic happen.

Who is it for?

Even by reading iUI's own motto ("User Interface for WebApp development on iPhone-class devices"), we can get pretty much what the whole deal is about.

This framework will only support iPhone, iPod Touch, and possibly iPad. That's about it.

How does it look?

After having written some code, here is how a typical iUI-based application looks:

What should I remember?

A few things are worth remembering about iUI:

- Extends standard HTML.
- Overrides links and forms with AJAX.
- No JavaScript knowledge required. Not necessarily a pro, as it comes handy in most cases.
- No theming (yet).
- Limited functionality.

iWebKit

The description of the framework we can find tells us almost anything we need to know about the package.

iWebKit is a file package designed to help you create your own iPhone, iPod Touch, and iPad compatible website or webapp. The kit is accessible to anyone, even people without any HTML knowledge, and is simple to understand, thanks to the included tutorials. In a couple of minutes, you will have created a full and professional looking website. iWebKit is a great tool because it is very easy to use, extremely fast, compatible, and extendable.

Who is it for?

iWebKit is aimed those non-developers who need to create a professional looking website or a interesting mobile web application from scratch.

The framework officially supports the iPhone family of devices, thus including iPod Touch and iPad, or any other platform running a WebKit-based browser.

How does it look?

Sample web applications submitted by iWebKit users are shown in the following screenshot:

What should I remember?

Some easy things to remember:

- Simple and minimalistic
- Mature (version 4)

- Provides support for WebKit only
- Easy-to-use

Comparison

After a quick overview of four (jQTouch, Sencha Touch, iUI, and iWebKit) packages with a goal similar to jQuery Mobile's, we can finally make a real comparison and understand which tool suits our needs better.

Even though some of the above-mentioned frameworks have already been available for quite a long time and jQuery Mobile is a new-born solution, the latter looks like the one which will get the biggest share of the market, also thanks to the (financial) support gathered from its sponsors. And these are somewhat big sponsors: Mozilla, Nokia, Blackberry, Palm, and so on.

It's true, however, that jQuery Mobile is still in its early stages, with their first stable release only dating back to the beginning of November 2010 . The project has a great backing, though; a good share of the jQuery community is more than interested in the future developments of the project and is following closely the bug fixing and maintenance activities required in order to offer a valuable product which can stand the test of time.

Type of package comparison

Let's start off by saying that, in terms of weight, Sencha Touch is out of the game already. Due to its nature (a standalone package), it cannot compete with any other product, being over 120kb, considering the weight and poor optimization of JQuery for mobile devices; John Resig and the development team were motivated to create a mobile version that spots the issues with jQTouch.

The excellent performances and reduced file size of jQuery Mobile is mainly due to the joint efforts of the jQuery developers to create a mobile version of the popular JavaScript library, already lightweight and extremely customizable and expandable.

As for appearance, the only way iUI can be modified is by editing the CSS code (even though the latest version can be customized with themes). The other three frameworks taken into account have a more or less advanced theming system that can be, in most cases, compared to jQuery Mobile's though the integration and overall consistency of the latter is just a better comparison of supported devices

Needless to say, jQuery Mobile is a long way ahead of the others.

However, it should be noted that some of the libraries presented in the previous section have been developed with the sole purpose of enabling iPhone developers to build powerful web application for iPhone-like devices. This is the case with iUI, for example, whose website clearly states that the project aims to make iUI a sort of default UI language for iPhone-class devices.

On the other hand, jQuery Mobile has a table (Mobile Graded Browser Support, located at `http://jquerymobile.com/gbs/`) which lists a series of mobile platforms and mobile browsers.

To each combination is assigned a grade (A, B, or C), which is "a combination of the browser quality combined with the browser's relevance in the larger mobile market":

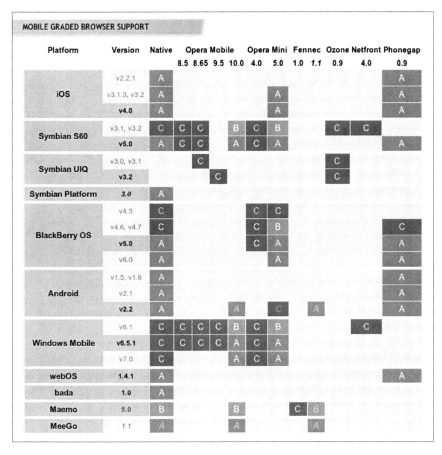

MOBILE GRADED BROWSER SUPPORT

Platform	Version	Native	Opera Mobile 8.5	8.65	9.5	10.0	Opera Mini 4.0	5.0	Fennec 1.0	1.1	Ozone 0.9	Netfront 4.0	Phonegap 0.9
iOS	v2.2.1	A											A
	v3.1.3, v3.2	A						A					A
	v4.0	A						A					A
Symbian S60	v3.1, v3.2	C	C	C	B		C	B			C	C	
	v5.0	A	C	C			A	C	A				A
Symbian UIQ	v3.0, v3.1				C							C	
	v3.2					C						C	
Symbian Platform	3.0	A											
BlackBerry OS	v4.5	C					C	C					
	v4.6, v4.7	C					C	B					C
	v5.0	A					C	A					A
	v6.0	A						A					A
Android	v1.5, v1.6	A											A
	v2.1	A											A
	v2.2	A				A		C	A				A
Windows Mobile	v6.1	C	C	C	C	B	C	B				C	
	v6.5.1	C	C	C	C	A	C	A					
	v7.0	C				A	C	A					
webOS	1.4.1	A											A
bada	1.0	A											
Maemo	5.0	B				B			C	B			
MeeGo	1.1	A				A			A				

jQuery Mobile is working to support all A grade browsers. This means that we will be actively testing against those browsers and ensuring that they work as best as they possibly can. The browsers will receive the full jQuery Mobile CSS and JavaScript (although the ultimate layout may be a gracefully degraded version of the full capabilities, depending upon the browser).

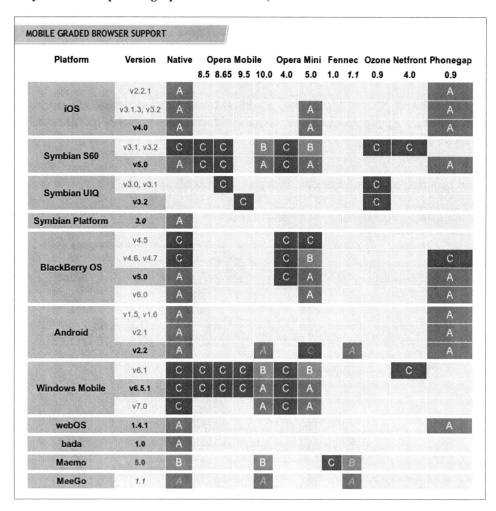

MOBILE GRADED BROWSER SUPPORT

Platform	Version	Native	Opera Mobile				Opera Mini		Fennec		Ozone	Netfront	Phonegap
			8.5	8.65	9.5	10.0	4.0	5.0	1.0	1.1	0.9	4.0	0.9
iOS	v2.2.1	A											A
	v3.1.3, v3.2	A						A					A
	v4.0	A						A					A
Symbian S60	v3.1, v3.2	C	C	C			B	C	B		C	C	
	v5.0	A	C	C			A	C	A				A
Symbian UIQ	v3.0, v3.1				C						C		
	v3.2					C					C		
Symbian Platform	3.0	A											
BlackBerry OS	v4.5	C					C	C					
	v4.6, v4.7	C					C	B					C
	v5.0	A					C	A					A
	v6.0	A						A					A
Android	v1.5, v1.6	A											A
	v2.1	A											A
	v2.2	A				A		C	A				A
Windows Mobile	v6.1	C	C	C	C	C	B	C	B			C	
	v6.5.1	C	C	C	C	C	A	C	A				
	v7.0	C					A	C	A				
webOS	1.4.1	A											A
bada	1.0	A											
Maemo	5.0	B			B				C	B			
MeeGo	1.1	A			A					A			

Grades can be broken down in this manner:

- A – High Quality: A browser that's capable of, at minimum, utilizing media queries (a requirement for jQuery Mobile). These browsers will be actively tested against, but may not receive the full capabilities of jQuery Mobile.

- B – Medium Quality: A capable browser that doesn't have enough market share to warrant day-to-day testing. Bug fixes will still be applied to help these browsers.

- C – Low Quality: A browser that is not capable of utilizing media queries. They won't be provided any jQuery Mobile scripting or CSS (falling back to plain HTML and simple CSS).

Why choose jQuery Mobile?

Developers are now able to create applications that will run on a number of different platforms, not only those considered top-notch (that is, iOS and Android). jQuery Mobile is built around the principle of progressive enhancement, meaning any jQuery Mobile application will work in many browsers, even those that don't support JavaScript (that is, Windows Mobile), thanks to graceful degradation techniques.

This task is accomplished thanks to graceful degradation, so the browsers that do not support the set of features provided by jQuery Mobiles.

Accessibility and simplicity also play a key role in the development of both the jQuery Mobile library and applications built with its aid, the framework being completely mark-up driven (it requires no JavaScript configuration) and ARIA accessible. This is to say, basically, that jQuery Mobile is easy to get started with and makes it possible to navigate the pages using a keyboard – when working on a desktop computer.

Importantly, not to be forgotten is the small file size, specifically considered for mobile usage: as of the end of 2010, the Alpha version of jQuery Mobile weighs around 12KB and makes little use of images, preferring icons and heavy usage of CSS (6KB).

The modularity of the library also allows for a comprehensive theming system, very effective, for which a Themeroller tool is scheduled for the final 1.0 release.

In the end, it all comes down to our requirements and needs.

If we were to prefer a minimalist approach and we only needed to provide support for a handful of mobile platforms (iPhone), we'd likely be happy using any of the frameworks mentioned earlier.

But if – and this is the case – we care for cross-platform compatibility, ease-of-use, and some sort of consistency for a top-notch browsing experience, we're more likely to choose jQuery Mobile as our tool of choice in any mobile application we're going to develop.

How to get jQuery mobile

There should be no problems at all obtaining a copy of jQuery Mobile, but anyway, here is a quick walkthrough to get all the mobile development enthusiasts out there started.

The fastest, easiest way to include jQuery Mobile into your website is by downloading one of the CDN-hosted versions that the jQuery Mobile project provides, which include images as well.

You can choose from two types of packages to download: one is uncompressed and for debugging purposes only (very large size); the other one is the minified and gzipped set of files which are ready to deploy.

 jQuery Mobile 1.0 Alpha 2 requires jQuery 1.4.4, which can be download from `http://docs.jquery.com/Downloading_jQuery`.

CDN-hosted JavaScript can be obtained from:

- `jquery-mobile-1.0a2.js` (Uncompressed, 102KB, useful for debugging) `http://code.jquery.com/mobile/1.0a2/jquery.mobile-1.0a2.js`.
- `jquery-mobile-1.0a2.min.js` (Minified and gzipped, 13KB, ready to deploy) `http://code.jquery.com/mobile/1.0a2/jquery.mobile-1.0a2.min.js`.

CDN-hosted CSS can be downloaded from:

- `jquery-mobile-1.0a2.css` (Uncompressed, 49KB, useful for debugging) `http://code.jquery.com/mobile/1.0a2/jquery.mobile-1.0a2.css`.
- `jquery-mobile-1.0a2.min.css` (Minified and gzipped, 6KB, ready to deploy) `http://code.jquery.com/mobile/1.0a2/jquery.mobile-1.0a2.min.css`.

A Zip file is also available for those willing to host the files themselves. The Zip file contains both versions of the JavaScript library (uncompressed and minified), all the required images, and CSS instructions, and can be downloaded from the following URL:

- `jquery-mobile-1.0a2.zip` (Zip file: JavaScript, CSS, and images) `http://code.jquery.com/mobile/1.0a2/jquery.mobile-1.0a2.zip`.

If you have chosen to make use of the CDN-hosted versions, the following couple of lines of code can be used to link to the libraries and the CSS stylesheet needed to set up jQuery Mobile:

```
<link rel="stylesheet" href="http://code.jquery.com/mobile/1.0a2/
jquery.mobile-1.0a2.min.css" />
<script src="http://code.jquery.com/jquery-1.4.4.min.js"></script>
<script src="http://code.jquery.com/mobile/1.0a2/jquery.mobile-1.0a2.
min.js"></script>
```

 You can use the preceding code to link to your self-hosted libraries or code snippets by changing the `src` address.

jQuery Mobile in action

The whole jQuery Mobile documentation is built using jQuery Mobile itself, as you can see at http://jquerymobile.com/demos/1.0a3/.

Reading through the documentation pages should give you a clear understanding of how jQuery Mobile works and looks out of the box. There are, of course, ways to make it look different, change the color scheme and everything else, but its feel won't change.

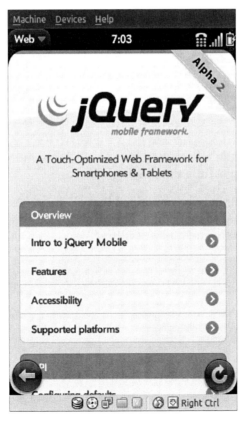

Now, scroll to the very bottom of the page. Can you see the **jQuery API browser** link under the **Demos** section?

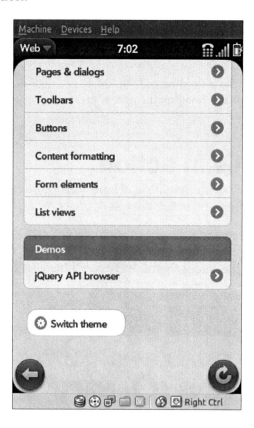

Well, this is a slightly more advanced example of jQuery Mobile in action, and it might be worth spending a little time toying with it.

For example, you may already have noticed that all the pages belonging to the jQuery API browser share some details. The most obvious one is the top bar, which reports the page title and a **back** button.

Also, all pages are presented as a list of links and have a **Switch theme** button at the bottom:

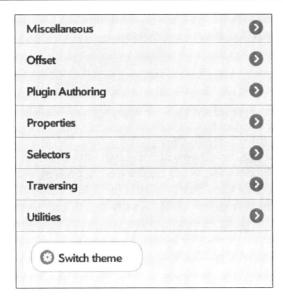

These are some of the elements we will be able to incorporate into our web pages and which will be shown in the very same way in all mobile browsers.

Getting involved

The great thing about open source software is that anyone can take it, play with it for a while, and redistribute it.

However, our objective here is far from copying the whole jQuery library, change a couple of lines, and pass it off as our own – but rather, we have the opportunity to contribute to the jQuery Mobile source and help improve the functioning of our beloved JavaScript file.

Unfortunately, we still are to mess around with the first alpha release, and bugs will be with us for a while, no matter which platform we choose. But this gives us the chance to help out and get involved in the active development of jQuery Mobile!

For example, a very simple yet helpful task is to file bugs in the jQuery Mobile Bug Tracker (`https://github.com/jquery/jquery-mobile/issues`). As of now, there are over 200 issues reported and looking for someone to take care of them.

In fact, if you think you are competent enough at fixing bugs, adding some extra functionalities, or even just correcting non-working code, you can provide patches in the jQuery Mobile Source Repository through GitHub (`https://github.com/jquery/jquery-mobile/`) or discuss the code on the jQuery Mobile Development Forum (`http://forum.jquery.com/developing-jquery-mobile`).

A live code test is available at `http://jquerymobile.com/test/`, pulling directly from the latest commit in the source repository.

Summary

In this chapter, we have had a first taste of what jQuery Mobile is like.

Its features are great, indeed, even compared to some of the libraries that are available and under active development for quite some time now: cross-browser compatibility on mobile devices, small size, theming system, and increased simplicity are only a few of the enhancements the jQuery Mobile team made to the standard jQuery library in order to create a fully-functional mobile library.

The next chapter will deal with getting started with jQuery Mobile and finally we will see how to create our first few pages for everybody to see.

2
Organizing Content: Pages and Dialogs

This chapter will deal with creating and organizing pages and dialogs, which are used to display our content using the tools jQuery Mobile has to offer.

The jQuery Mobile framework has a particular way of handling pages – and displays them – so it's best to learn how to properly set them up and then fill them with content (that is, buttons, forms, links, and so on).

The basic page structure is, actually, very simple: as jQuery Mobile is focused on ease-of-use, very little code is required in order to get a fully-working basic page online.

Specifically, we're going to cover:

- Understanding page structure
- How multi-page templates work
- How to link internal and external pages
- Navigation and page transition in AJAX
- Dialogs: creation, deletion, and behavior
- Theming pages and dialogs

Understanding page structure

The jQuery Mobile page structure is based on the HTML5 standard, and is optimized to make use of most of its tags, attributes, and elements out of the box.

At this point, one may ask what the problem is if we can follow HTML5 directives and code the page like we have always done until now.

The reason we must take a close look at how jQuery Mobile processes the pages and their standard layout is because the frameworks needs and recognizes some elements depending on some attributes we have to specify.

So, there are a couple of things to bear in mind:

1. Any jQuery Mobile page must start with an HTML5 doctype, so we can get the best out of the framework.

   ```
   <!DOCTYPE html>
   ```

2. Tags such as `<html>`, `<head>`, `<title>`, and `<body>` still serve their goal, and must be included in the code.

3. In the `<head>`, references to the jQuery Mobile stylesheet, jQuery, and jQuery Mobile are required.

 Your link to jQuery and jQuery Mobile can point to either a CDN-hosted version or a locally stored version of the library.

4. Most importantly, any valid HTML markup can be used. Don't forget!

 Tags such as HEAD, BODY, DOCTYPE, and so on are not necessary in page fragments loaded programmatically by the jQuery framework, while they are required for validation purposes in other instances.

jQuery Mobile makes use of the custom data attributes (`http://dev.w3.org/html5/spec/elements.html#custom-data-attribute`) that let us add any attribute we like to an element.

This is to say, each element we introduce into our pages must have a data-role attribute specified, which helps jQuery Mobile identify the element(s) in which to find the content/markup.

We will then have a div whose `data-role` is set to `page`, which will work as our page. Inside the "page", we may add three optional containers: `header`, `content`, and `footer`.

 Although the inner divs (`header`, `content`, and `footer`) are not required in order to create a "page", you may want to include at least the "content" as the div in which all the page content is contained.

So, how do we create a page?

As we've already stated previously, jQuery Mobile needs the HTML5 doctype and links to jQuery and jQuery Mobile. And don't forget the jQuery Mobile stylesheet!

 We can link to CDN-hosted versions of both libraries to make things work smoother and easier – we don't have the hassle of downloading/uploading anything. However, if we are concerned with our application not working offline (or on an airplane without internet connection), we may want to download both jQuery libraries.
As links to CDN-hosted versions will be constantly changing to be updated to the latest version, we will link to a locally hosted version of the libraries.
Make sure you use the latest version available in your applications!

```
<!DOCTYPE html>
<html>
  <head>
    <title>jQuery Mobile Page Structure Test</title>
    <link rel="stylesheet" href="jquery.mobile-latest.min.css"" />
    <script src="jquery-latest.min.js"></script>
    <script src="jquery.mobile-latest.min.js"></script>
  </head>
  <body>
  </body>
</html>
```

We can then add the page div to the `<body>`. Each page can be identified by an ID property, which is often set to home if we're building the home page:

```
<div data-role="page" id="home">
  <div data-role="header">
  </div>
  <div data-role="content">
  </div>
  <div data-role="footer">
  </div>
</div>
```

The last step is to add some content to the page, and see how the page looks on a mobile device:

```
<div data-role="page" id="home">
  <div data-role="header">
    <h1>Home page</h1>
  </div>

  <div data-role="content">
    <p>Hello Mobile World!</p>
  </div>

  <div data-role="footer">
    <h4>I'm the footer</h4>
  </div>
</div>
```

This is the complete code for the HTML page:

```
<!DOCTYPE html>
<html>
  <head>
    <title>jQuery Mobile Page Structure Test</title>
    <link rel="stylesheet" href="jquery.mobile-latest.min.css" />
    <script src="jquery-latest.min.js"></script>
    <script src="jquery.mobile-latest.min.js"></script>
  </head>
  <body>
    <div data-role="page" id="home">
      <div data-role="header">
        <h1>Home page</h1>
      </div>

      <div data-role="content">
        <p>Hello Mobile World!</p>
      </div>

      <div data-role="footer">
        <h4>I'm the footer</h4>
      </div>
    </div>
  </body>
</html>
```

And here is the page as it shows from our markup:

You can add a `data-position="fixed"` attribute to the header or footer in order to make sure they always stay, respectively, at the top or bottom of the screen.

How multi-page templates work

In addition to the simple, and more straightforward, single page layout we have just had a look at, jQuery Mobile allows for an easy-to-implement multi-page template which basically lets us create pages within pages.

To better understand how this multi-page thing is supposed to work, we must understand that a jQuery Mobile calls "page" a portion of code that represents a page.

In each HTML file, we can then include more than one "page", resulting in the browser fetching only one page and offering a smoother experience to the user.

The "page" which will show by default is the first one (that is, the one that comes first in the code).

Our "pages" are identified by their id attribute, which we can set to the outermost div of each "page", which also needs the data-role attribute to be set to page.

For example, we can try to create a jQuery Mobile site which has three pages (**home** page, **about** page, and **contact** page) all contained in a single HTML file called index.html.

The standard layout for a single page is not modified, so we just copy over our basic page structure from the previous example:

```
<!DOCTYPE html>
<html>
  <head>
    <title>jQuery Mobile Page Structure Test</title>
    <link rel="stylesheet" href="jquery.mobile-latest.min.css" />
    <script src="jquery-latest.min.js"></script>
    <script src="jquery.mobile-latest.min.js"></script>
  </head>
  <body>
    <div data-role="page" id="home">
      <div data-role="header">
        <h1>Home page</h1>
      </div>
      <div data-role="content">
        <p>Hello Mobile World!</p>
      </div>
      <div data-role="footer">
        <h4>I'm the footer</h4>
      </div>
    </div>
  </body>
</html>
```

Next, we add the other two pages using the same technique we create the home page with. Simply, a div with a data-role attribute of page will tell jQuery Mobile to process the element as a page.

Make sure to put the markup for the other two "pages" after the home "page", so the latter will be visible by default:

```
<div data-role="page" id="about">
  <div data-role="header">
    <h1>About us</h1>
  </div>

  <div data-role="content">
    <p>Lorem ipsum dolor.</p>
  </div>

  <div data-role="footer">
    <p>I'm the footer</p>
  </div>
</div>

<div data-role="page" id="contact">
  <div data-role="header">
    <h1>Contact</h1>
  </div>

  <div data-role="content">
    <p>Drop us an email!</p>
  </div>

  <div data-role="footer">
    <h4>I'm the footer</h4>
  </div>
</div>
```

Finally, here is the complete code:

```
<!DOCTYPE html>
<html>
  <head>
    <title>jQuery Mobile Page Structure Test</title>

    <link rel="stylesheet" href="jquery.mobile-latest.min.css" />

    <script src="jquery-latest.min.js"></script>
    <script src="jquery.mobile-latest.min.js"></script>

  </head>

  <body>
    <div data-role="page" id="home">
      <div data-role="header">
        <h1>Home page</h1>
      </div>

      <div data-role="content">
        <p>Hello Mobile World!</p>
      </div>
```

```
        <div data-role="footer">
          <p>I'm the footer</p>
        </div>
      </div>

      <div data-role="page" id="about">
        <div data-role="header">
          <h1>About us</h1>
        </div>

        <div data-role="content">
          <p>Lorem ipsum dolor</p>
        </div>

        <div data-role="footer">
          <p>I'm the footer</p>
        </div>
      </div>

      <div data-role="page" id="contact">
        <div data-role="header">
          <h1>Contact</h1>
        </div>

        <div data-role="content">
          <p>Drop us an email!</p>
        </div>

        <div data-role="footer">
          <h4>I'm the footer</h4>
        </div>
      </div>
    </body>
  </html>
```

But how can we access the newly created pages?

Well, to access the home "page", we only need to load the page: it will show by default.
As for the other two "pages", we can either link to them from any page in our application (read the next section about linking) or just add #about or #contact to the URL in order to view, respectively the **about** or **contact** "pages".

For example, we can link to the contact page by using the following code:

```
<a href="#contact">Click here to go to the contact page</a>
```

The point of having several pages in the same HTML file is that, for small sites, the latency between the client server and the overhead from the HTTP protocol slows down the site more than the marginal increase in bandwidth used by including the extra pages in a single file.

Keep in mind this is one of the reasons we need to supply an `id` attribute to the "pages" we create.

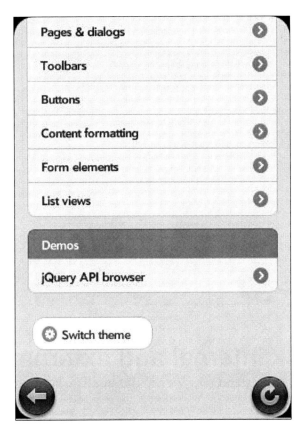

You may have noticed a back button has appeared. By clicking the back button, jQuery Mobile brings you back to the previous page.

How to link internal and external pages

First of all, we must understand how we can differentiate between internal and external pages.

Internal pages are those pages whose domain is the same as the currently displayed pages.

Obviously, external pages are pages whose domain is anything but the one we're currently browsing or that have `rel="external"` or target attributes.

For example, let's say we are visiting the page `http://example.com/mobile.html` and we have the following elements:

Link markup	Link type
`<a href="http://example.com/home.html">`	Internal
`<a href="http://example.com/home.html#about">`	Internal
`<a href="http://example.com/home.html" rel="external">`	External
`<a href="http://example.com/home.html" target="_blank">`	External
`<a href="http://google.com">`	External

The reason that jQuery Mobile makes this kind of separation lies in the way the framework handles the two types of link.

Whenever the library has to deal with internal links, they are "automatically turned into Ajax requests and displayed with an animated page transition by the framework".

Of course, the same cannot happen for external links, and thus they cause a complete page refresh.

 We have already discussed the possibility of linking to pages within the same HTML file by using the ID to which they are referenced as an anchor. This works for multi-page layouts only, beware!

Navigation and page transitioning in AJAX

We have already discussed the particular way in which jQuery Mobile "follows" links: rather than forcing the browser to open a new page, the framework makes use of AJAX to load the (internal) page into the existing page's DOM.

In this way, the AJAX requests not only makes the user experience smooth but also results in quicker responses to the requests: every time we want to load an internal page (that is, a portion of a page), we use AJAX to asynchronously request that particular piece of information instead of reloading the whole page from the server, thus resulting in a more pleasant user experience.

But since we are basically always on the same page, we may wonder how can we move back and forward in the history stack and reference to other pages?

The answer to this question is, however, quite complicated. However, before we start reasoning on the effective way jQuery Mobile handles change page requests; we must make clear that we can still bookmark any page on our website. How? Using URL **hashes**, jQuery Mobile ensures each page has its own, unique URL.

Any time a link (to an internal page) is clicked, jQuery Mobile does three things:

1. Prevents the default click behavior.
2. Requests the URL via AJAX.
3. Changes `location.hash` to the new page's relative URL.

The framework uses the `$.mobile.changePage` function (see section in *Chapter 3, Working with methods and utilities* or the jQuery Mobile documentation) to change from one page to a new page, be it internal (uses AJAX) or external (does not load into existing DOM).

The `$.mobile.changePage` function handles all the logic and processes required to deal with page changes and, as such, is also responsible for applying transition effects once the requested page has finished loading into the existing DOM.

Page transitions can be specified case by case, adding the `data-transition` attribute to the link. Valid values for the transition are the following:

Value	Effect
slide	Slide right to left, or left to right if going back.
slideup	Slide from bottom to top, or top to bottom if going back.
slidedown	Slide from top to bottom, or bottom to top if going back.
pop	Expand, or contract if going back.
fade	Fade in, or fade out if going back.
flip	Flip in, or flip out if going back.

The default page transition (slide) applies in any case no other transition has been specified, and can be modified through the `$.mobile.defaultTransition` option.

 You can force a backwards transition by adding a `data-back="true"` attribute to the link.

Surprisingly, page transitions are all driven by CSS rules, and the `$.mobile.changePage` function just applies and removes CSS classes to the two "pages" that are involved in the page transition.

For example, consider a *slideup* transition, with two pages involved: the **exiting** page and the entering page.

The exiting page would be given the classes `slideup` and `out`, whereas the entering page would be given the classes `ui-page-active`, `slideup`, and `in`. Also, the `ui-page-active` class, which identifies the currently active page, would be removed from the exiting page. Once the animation is complete, the classes `out` and `in` would be removed from, respectively, the exiting and the entering pages.

To sum it up, the following points pretty much reflect what goes on, internally, every time a link is clicked:

1. Check if links to an either internal or external page.
2. If an internal link with no `rel="external"` or `target` attributes specified is detected, make an AJAX request for the URL; just change page otherwise (no more processing).
3. Set `location.hash` to the new page's relative URL to allow bookmarking and referencing.
4. Apply transition effect: remove the `ui-page-active` class from the exiting page and add it to the entering page; add transition class, and `out` and `in` classes to, respectively, exiting and entering pages.

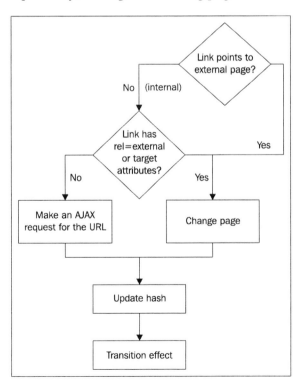

Dialogs: creation, deletion, and behavior

As simple as it sounds, a dialog is nothing but a standard page styled differently: the jQuery Mobile documentation points out that *"the framework adds styles to add rounded corners, margins around the page and a dark background to make the dialog appear to be suspended above the page"*.

To create a dialog, we just have to specify the `data-rel="dialog"` attribute in the link, pretty much like the following example:

```
<a href="dialog.html" data-rel="dialog">Dialog!</a>
```

As dialogs are standard pages, the default slide transition (or whatever you changed it to) will be used, unless we do not specify otherwise:

```
<a href="dialog.html" data-rel="dialog" data-
transition="pop">Dialog!</a>
```

Usually, the pop transition is used as the standard dialog transition due to the animation, which looks like a new window is, well, popping up.

 Links that create dialogs use the `$.mobile.changePage` function to open a page without updating the hash, which is useful for keeping dialogs out of history tracking.

Furthermore, there are two ways to close a dialog, depending on what we are trying to achieve.

If we need to programmatically close a dialog via JavaScript, we can use jQuery to select the dialog to be closed, and then call the close method:

```
$('.ui-dialog').dialog ('close');
```

If, on the other hand, we are just worried about how to return to the previous page, we can either rely on the **Close** button on the top-left corner of the dialog (visible by default) or add a cancel/back/close button that links to the previous page.

Theming pages and dialogs

We have already had a quick glance at jQuery Mobile's theming mechanism, but purposely kept the explanation at a general level.

We're now focusing on how to specifically modify the look and feel of our pages and dialogs, making use of the jQuery Mobile theme framework, which allows for a great level of customization of our web application.

Actually, as pages are composed of many other elements (buttons, forms, sliders, forms, and so on), this still is a generalization, as single widgets will be discussed in greater detail once we learn how to use and include them in our application.

The default theme makes use of colors from various swatches, and we have already seen it in action in the previous chapters. This is what our web application looks like if no modifications to the theme have been done:

We can then change some of the swatches, even for individual items.

The data-theme attribute can be applied to the header of footer, or even to the whole "page". For example, we may want to change the header so it has a yellow background (Swatch E).

It's important to note the themes cascade, because if you apply a theme to the content element, it will also apply to all elements within that div element.

1. The header consists of the following code, and we have to replace it with another line of code that modifies the default color scheme:

```
<div data-role="header">
  <h1>Default Header</h1>
</div>
```

2. We change the swatch by adding the data-theme attribute to the header container:

```
<div data-role="header" data-theme="e">
  <h1>Swatch E Header</h1>
</div>
```

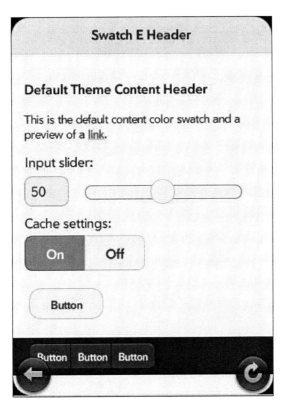

3. The same applies to any other element we wish to style differently, although it is recommended not to style directly the content container, as it would result in different background colors in the same page.
    Instead, we can add the data-theme attribute to the page container, so that the whole page has a consistent look (Swatch A follows):

```
<div data-role="page" id="home" data-theme="a">
  <!-- header, content, footer to be put here -->
</div>
```

Other Swatches can be applied to the page so that it looks similar to one of the following color schemes.

A Swatch B themed page has blue as its primary color:

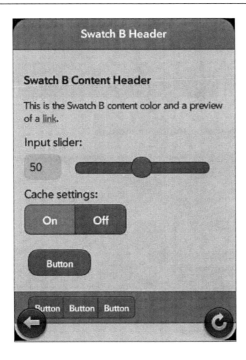

Swatch C is off-white:

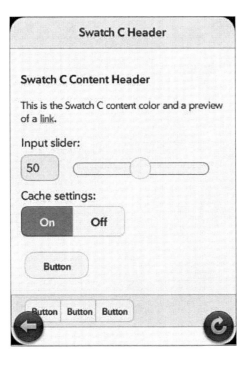

Swatch D resembles the Swatch C look, but has gray undertones to make the header and footer stand out more:

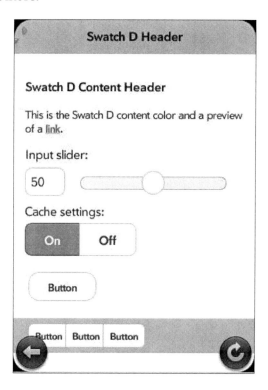

Finally, Swatch E is yellow-based:

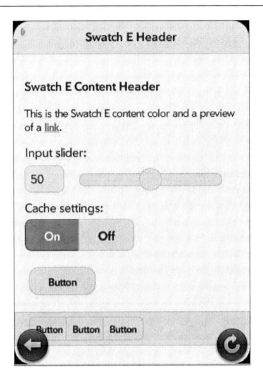

As for dialogs, as they are in no way different from standard pages, if not for some further styling automatically applied by the framework, the way in which we change the theme is exactly the same.

However, there is one thing we may want to do to enhance or increase the number of possibilities we have with dialogs.

If we plan on using a dialog to give the user a selection of actions to choose from, we could remove the header portion of the dialog so it displays in a way better-suited to look like a control sheet:

```
<div data-role="page">
  <div data-role="content" data-theme="a">
    <h3>Share Photos</h3>

    <a href="action.html" data-role="button" data-theme="b">Email</a>
    <a href="action.html" data-role="button" data-theme="b">Upload to
flickr</a>
    <a href="action.html" data-role="button" data-theme="b">Share on
Facebook</a>
    <a href="action.html" data-role="button" data-theme="b">Tweet
photo</a>z
```

```
        <a href="action.html" data-role="button" data-rel="back" data-
theme="a">Cancel</a>
  </div>
</div>
```

The following dialog, from the jQuery Mobile documentation pages, presents the user with multiple buttons asking for a way to share photos. The **Cancel** button should be included this time, as there is no **Close** button in the top-left corner, as we removed the header:

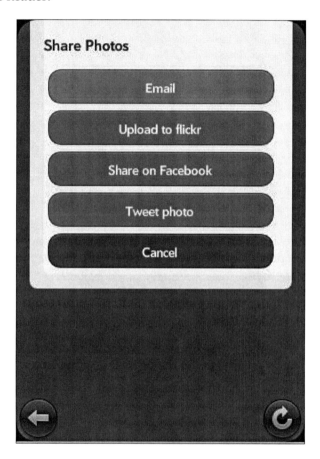

Summary

In this chapter, we have learned how to properly create and modify pages using jQuery Mobile. The subtle difference that differentiates real pages from "pages" (or "views") that are contained into a single HTML file gives us two options from which we can choose from when we're about to develop our web applications.

However, we have to carefully take into account the pros and cons of every method, since using a single page and creating dozens of "views" would result in poor usability issues, to say the least.

Theming plays a central role in jQuery Mobile, and a lot of options are available to further customize our web applications.

For example, we will see, in the next chapter, how to effectively change the default configuration of jQuery Mobile, and how we can handle events and make use of the built-in methods and functions to better control how our web applications behave.

Configuring and Extending jQuery Mobile

In the previous chapter, we had a quick look at the new jQuery Mobile framework in terms of aesthetics, improvements, and how well it performs against other libraries of the same type.

We are now slowly moving towards the point at which we start putting into practice what we've learned until now, and experiment with what we have at hand.

jQuery Mobile is a very flexible framework and, even though its cross-compatibility efforts may sound like some sort of limitation, you will be amazed by the number of different things you can do with jQuery Mobile.

But before we take off and start creating a simple mobile page, we must make sure a couple of things are clear in our minds.

In this chapter, we'll be dealing with:

- Customizing default settings
- Handling events
- Working with methods and utilities
- Using the theme framework

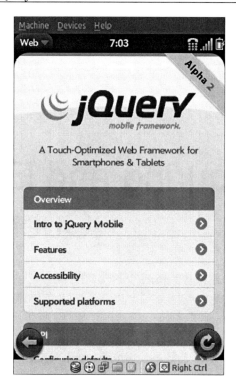

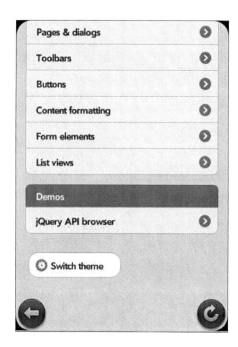

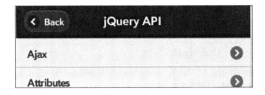

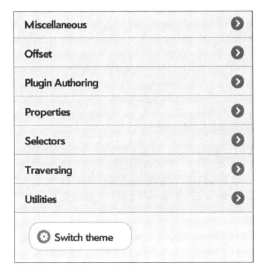

Customizing default settings

The first problem you may run into is jQuery Mobile configuration.

For example, you may not like its default CSS transition, or just need a different class to be attached to an active button, and so on.

jQuery Mobile, unlike the other jQuery projects (jQuery and jQuery UI), automatically applies some markup enhancements on loading. This means, obviously, that there are some settings, by default, that, while working fine for most, may not match your needs or desire.

Luckily, the default configuration jQuery Mobile comes with can be easily configured to suit your likings:

- jQuery Mobile triggers the `mobileinit` event on the `document` object immediately upon execution, so you can bind to it and override any default configuration:

```
$(document).bind ("mobileinit", function () {
```

```
    // here we can override the default configuration
});
```

- We can now change the default settings for some options modifying the corresponding $.mobile object using either jQuery's $.extend method or by specifying them individually.
  The $.mobile object is intended to store various configurable properties:

```
$(document).bind ("mobileinit", function () {
  $.extend ($.mobile, {
    option1: value1,
    option2: value2
  });

  $.mobile.option3 = value3;
});
```

> To understand how the $.extend function works, please read the jQuery API documentation at http://api.jquery.com/jQuery.extend/.
>
> To sum it up, though, it *merge[s] the contents of two or more objects together into the first object*" and returns the resulting object.

- But obviously, we need to know what settings we are allowed to modify via the $.mobile object.

- We can find a list of these options on the jQuery Mobile website, which is reported here with a little explanation.

- activeBtnClass
  string; default: "ui-btn-active"
    The class used for the "active" button state, from CSS framework.

- activePageClass
  string; default: "ui-page-active"
    The class used for the "active" page state, from CSS framework.

- ajaxFormsEnabled
  boolean; default: true
    jQuery Mobile will automatically handle form submissions through Ajax, when possible.

- ajaxLinksEnabled
  boolean; default: true
    jQuery Mobile will automatically handle link clicks through Ajax, when possible.

- `defaultTransition`
  string; default: 'slide'
  Set the default transition for page changes that use Ajax. Set to 'none' for no transitions by default.

- `gradeA`
  function that returns a boolean; default: a function returning the value of `$.support.mediaquery`
  Any support conditions that must be met in order to proceed.

- `hashListeningEnabled`
  boolean; default: true
  Automatically handle `location.hash` changes.

- `loadingMessage`
  string; default: "loading"
  Set the text that appears when a page is loading. If set to false, the message will not appear at all.

- `metaViewportContent`
  string; default: "width=device-width, minimum-scale=1, maximum-scale=1"
  Configure the auto-generated meta viewport tag's content attribute. If false, no meta tag will be appended to the DOM.

- `nonHistorySelectors`
  string; default: "dialog"
  Anchor links with a data-rel attribute value, or pages with a data-role value that match these selectors will not be trackable in history (they won't update the location.hash and won't be bookmarkable).

- `ns`
  string; default: ""
  The namespace used in data attributes. It's appended to the data- text, so it's better if you include a trailing dash so it looks like `data-mynamespace-role`.

- `pageLoadErrorMessage`
  string; default: "Error Loading Page"
  Text to appear when a page fails to load.

- `subPageUrlKey`
  string; default: "ui-page"
  The URL parameter used for referencing widget-generated sub-pages (such as those generated by nested listviews). Translates to *example.html&ui-page=subpageIdentifier*. The hash segment before &ui-page= is used by the framework for making an Ajax request to the URL where the sub-page exists.

Some of the above-mentioned properties can also be changed at runtime and for a particular instance of the event. For example, we might want a particular page, and only that page, to transit to the next page using a fade effect.

This changes the behavior of that transition only, and does not affect the default behavior of any other page we may change through this process of configuration.

Linking to jQuery Mobile

Pay close attention to the order in which you link to your JavaScript libraries, which is of maximum importance.

Always remember to link to jQuery Core first, then to jQuery Mobile.

But also make sure that, if you wish to change the default settings using the above-mentioned proceedings, your event handler before jQuery Mobile is loaded, due to the `mobileinit` event triggered right at execution.

The following is the recommended way to link to your JavaScript files:

```
<script src="jquery.js"></script>
<script src="custom-scripting.js"></script>
<script src="jquery-mobile.js"></script>
```

Handling events

You can still use any jQuery event you might need, but chances are you are looking forward to providing a better user experience to mobile users.

In order to enhance the performance of mobile-browsing, jQuery Mobile adds a new set of events which are mobile-specific and are based upon native events.

The custom set of events behaves no differently as any other jQuery event would, and can be bound to them with either `bind()` or `live()`.

Bind or live?

Both events are used for a similar purpose, which is attaching a handler to an event for the elements which match the current selector. The only difference is that `live()` attaches the handler to the elements matching the current selector that will be created in the future.

This is to say, for example, that if we want a click event to be bound to the already existing paragraphs only, we should use `bind()`.

On the other hand, if we plan on adding a new paragraph, and we need the click event handler attached to it, too, we need to use `live()` when binding the event handler.

Touch events

Touch events are those events triggered whenever the user touches any part of the page. Touch events are of different kinds, and are the primary way in which the user is supposed to interact with our web application.

These events even work on desktop computers, and you can "tap" and "swipe" with your mouse:

- Tap: Triggers any time after a complete touch event (that is, the users taps the on the element)
- Taphold: Triggers after the user touches the element and does not release for one second
- Swipe: Triggers when a horizontal drag of at least 30px occurs within one second
- Swipeleft: Triggers when the swipe event occurred in the left direction
- Swiperight: Triggers when the swipe event occurred in the right direction

To bind one of the above-mentioned events, we would proceed using the following code:

```
$('body').bind ('tap', function () {
  alert ('Tap!');
  return false;
});
```

Now, every time we tap on the page, a 'Tap!' alert will show, telling us the touch event has been correctly bound to the handler of our choice:

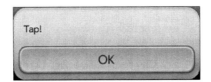

return false

You may be wondering why we added a return false line to our event handler, just like you may have seen in other snippets of code.

Well, in this case (empty page, just one event), it's pretty useless, but on a more cluttered application, the correct usage of this short line of code is of vital importance.

Returning false does three things, basically: `preventDefault()`, `stopPropagation()`, stops callback execution and returns immediately.

It's better not to misuse return false and use individually, when actually needed, the single methods.

Scroll events

Scroll events come into play whenever any type of scrolling is detected.

Due to the small size of mobile devices, pages always become quite long and there is an actual need to scroll down or up, left or right.

Please note that the functioning of this set of events is closely related to "swipe", as it's quite obvious that a scroll is obtained in the same way a swipe event is triggered, but vertically.

The difference here lies in how the two sets of events are processed. jQuery Mobile "does not have a vertical swipe event [yet] because that could interfere with scrolling". After all, "a vertical swipe event would be used on pages with no vertical scrolling and seems tricky to do with the wide range of devices which are now supported" (Todd Parker).

- scrollstart: Triggers when a scroll begins
- scrollstop: Triggers when a scroll finishes

The `scrollstart` event behaves strangely on OS devices, due to them freezing DOM manipulation when scroll starts. For this reason, any DOM manipulation is queued and applied when the scroll finishes, resulting in the `scrollstop` handler executing right after the `scrollstart` (delayed) one.

Page-related events

All other events that are in some way related to pages fall into this category.

Since jQuery Mobile allows for multi-page HTML files, we need to relyon a set of events which are triggered when a page is show or hidden, or created.

- `pageshow`: Triggers on the page being shown, after its transition completes.
- `pagehide`: Triggers on the page being hidden, after its transition completes.
- `pagebeforeshow`: Triggers on the page being shown, before its transition completes.
- `pagebeforehide`: XE "pagebeforehide event" Triggers on the page being hidden, before its transition completes.

 Note that whenever a page is shown or hidden, two events are triggered on that page. This means that, when a page transition occurs, there are actually four events triggered, depending on the page being shown (`pageshow` and `pagebeforeshow`) or hidden (**pagehide** and **pagebeforehide**).

A second argument in the callback function is provided in order to reference to either the next page (if the page on which the event is triggered is being shown) or the previous page (if the page is being hidden):

```
$('div').live ('pageshow',function (e, ui) {
  // ui.prevPage was just hidden
  // Object contains information about the hidden (previous) page
});

$('div').live ('pagehide',function (e, ui) {
  // ui.nextPage is showing
  // Object contains information about the current page
});
```

 The first page shown does not have a previous page reference, but an empty object is provided instead.

Page initialization also plays an important role in jQuery Mobile, primarily due to its auto-initializations of plugins based on markup convention found in a given page.

The jQuery Mobile documentation states that:

> *This auto-initialization is controlled by the "page" plugin, which dispatches events before and after it executes, allowing you to manipulate a page either pre-or-post initialization, or even provide your own initialization behavior and prevent the auto-initializations from occurring. Note that these events will only fire once per "page", as opposed to the show/hide events, which fire every time a page is shown and hidden.*

- `pagecreate`: Triggers on the page being initialized, after initialization completes

- `pagebeforecreate`: Triggers on the page being initialized, before initialization completes

 By binding to `pagebeforecreate` and returning `false`, you can prevent the page plugin from making its manipulations.

Note that for these events to be executed at page load, it is necessary we bind them before jQuery Mobile executes, in the `mobileinit` handler, as follows:

```
$(document).bind ("mobileinit", function () {
  // Here we override the default configuration
  // ...
  // Here we load the JS code we might need
  $('div[data-role*='page']').live ('pagecreate', function (e, ui) {
    // Call page event dispatcher / shared functions
  });
});
```

As we will see in the next chapter, the data-role attribute set to page lets us create multiple "pages" and wrap them into the same HTML file. We can then call the same functions every time a page is created, or write a script to differentiate between pages and run JavaScript code selectively (see Appendix).

If a change in the orientation of the device is detected, there is the possibility to change the page style, so we can display the page correctly at any time:

- `Orientationchange`: Triggers when the device orientation changes by turning it vertically or horizontally

To allow for an effective change of styling when the device orientation is modified, the callback function provides an orientation property which equals either portrait or landscape.

This value is also added as class to the HTML elements, so that you can write the CSS code accordingly.

For example, we might want to use the following CSS code to distinguish between portrait and landscape orientation:

```
.landscape img {
  // page is in landscape view, image should be wider
  width: 480px;
}

.portrait img {
  // page is in portrait view, image should be narrower
  width: 320px;
}
```

Actually, I found out that, if we bind the `orientationchange` event to the window object, we can work with the `window.orientation` property which behaves in the following way:

```
$(window).bind ('orientationchange', function (e) {
  $('body').removeClass ('portrait landscape').addClass (e.orientation
? 'landscape' : 'portrait');
});
```

The above code should also make sure the correct class is added to the body, so we can apply the right styling options.

The `window.orientation` property returns 0 for portrait and 90 or -90 for landscape view.

Another way to make sure the CSS code works correctly even on devices that do not interact well with the `orientation.change` event is using CSS code so that it distinguishes between page orientation itself:

```
@media all and (orientation: portrait) {
  body { background-color: red }
}
<link rel="stylesheet" media="all and (orientation: landscape)"
href="landscape.css" />
```

Working with methods and utilities

In addition to the set of properties we are able to configure as default options, jQuery mobile lets us make use of a set of methods which are of great aid in dealing with some common issues we may encounter during the creation of our web application.

These methods are all accessible through the `$.mobile` object (of which we will learn more as we go on) and can be called at any time in our script, depending on our needs.

> The `$.mobile.activePage` property refers to the page currently displayed.

- `addResolutionBreakpoints` (number | array values): Add width breakpoints to the min/max width classes that are added to the HTML element

- The values argument can be either a number or an array of numbers

> jQuery Mobile has defined a set of classes that are applied to the top-level element and updated on window load or resize.
>
> Breakpoints (that is, the widths at which the class is added) are set by default at the following widths: 320, 480, 768, 1024, and for each of these, two classes can be used: `min-width-XXXpx` and `max-width-XXXpx`, where XXX is a number belonging to the width breakpoints.

Width breakpoints can thus be manipulated (well, just added, that is) using the previously mentioned method, very similarly to the following example:

```
// A single width (number)...
$.mobile.addResolutionBreakpoints (800);

// ... Or more than one at the same time (array)
$.mobile.addResolutionBreakpoints ([800, 1440]);
```

The following classes will then be respectively added if the window width matches the newly created breakpoints: min-width-800px and max-width-800px, min-width-1440px and max-width-1440px:

- changePage (string | object | array to, string transition, boolean back, boolean changeHash)
  Programmatically changes from one page to another.

The `to` argument can be expressed in a variety of forms. Thanks to this feature, the developer can decide to provide it as: a simple string, which would represent the relative path to the page (that is, `'../contact.html'`); a jQuery object, representing a "page" contained in the same file (that is, `$('#contact')`); an array of two page references `[from, to]`, from transitioning from a known page (assumed as the currently active page `$.mobile.activePage`); an object to send form data, consisting of `{to: url, data: serialized form data, type: "get" or "post"}`.

The `back` and `changeHash` arguments, when set `true`, will respectively cause a reverse-direction transition and update the hash to the page's URL. They are respectively `false` and `true` by default. It is important to note that `changeHash` is necessary to keep history current in the browser.

 Transitions can be chosen from the following (default) list, which can be modified changing the default configuration through `$.mobile.transitions`: 'slide', 'slideup', 'slidedown', 'pop', 'flip', 'fade'.

There are several ways to change a page programmatically.

The simplest one is nothing more than the following code, which leaves the default transition (slide) and any other default configuration untouched. The page is tracked in history (that is, the back button links back to the page from which we came):

```
$.mobile.changePage ('../path/to/page.html');
```

A slightly more advanced approach can be obtained if we try to change the default transition effect and prevent the page from being tracked in history by setting the `changeHash` argument to false:

```
$.mobile.changePage ('other/page.html', 'fade', false, false);
```

Moreover, we can send form data along, passing an object as the first argument:

```
var pageData = { url: formresults.php, type: 'get', data:
$('form#myform').serialize () };
$.mobile.changePage (pageData);
```

We can also store a reference to a page into a variable so that, once we have reached another page, we can set use `changePage` to load a third page as if we came from the page for which we stored the reference:

```
var previousPage = $.mobile.activePage.data ('ui.prevPage');
// now navigate away, browse the other "pages"
// but make sure you are on another "page" before the next line is
triggered,
```

```
// which will make it look like the page we come from is previousPage.
//
// for example, you can $.mobile.changePage ($('#secondpage'),
'slideup')
$.mobile.changePage ([previousPage, anotherPreviousPage], 'pop');
```

`pageLoading` (boolean done): Shows (done set to true) or hides (default) the page loading message, which is configurable via `$.mobile.loadingMessage`.

Usage is as simple as it seems:

```
// To show the loading message
$.mobile.pageLoading ();

// To hide the loading message
$.mobile.pageLoading (true);
```

`silentScroll` (number yPos): Scrolls to a particular Y position (default is 0) without triggering scroll event listeners:

```
// Scroll to 100px
$.mobile.silentScroll (100);
```

Using the theme framework

Visually, jQuery mobile offers a range of themes that, by default, draw inspiration from a variety of UI elements and mix them all together to create an original, yet somewhat familiar, user experience.

Instead of trying to make the elements explicitly look like those from another library or framework, or trying to reproduce the feel of a popular mobile OS, jQuery Mobile defines a new set of looks and experiences for mobile applications.

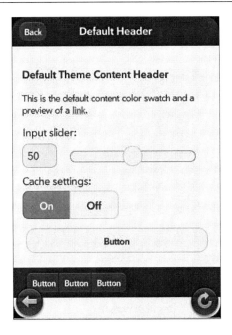

The default theme for jQuery Mobile looks very nice indeed, combining colors from two of the five swatches already available out of the box to apply to your web pages.

The theme framework implemented in jQuery Mobile relies on CSS3 specifications in order to reduce the page weight: rounded corners, box and text shadows, and gradients are all obtained making use of CSS3 properties.

The visual effects we are able to design combining "normal" CSS techniques and a bunch of these new properties can be packaged together in **themes**, which usually consist in not more than one CSS file. Each theme can contain up to 26 **color swatches**, each consisting of a header bar, content body, and button states, which can be freely mixed to create unique designs.

In the following screenshot, we can see the five swatches (a, b, c, d, and e) for buttons and bars and how they are applied and look like:

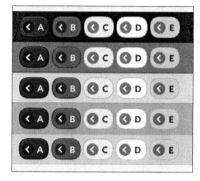

A set of icons is also included and can be used in a variety of situations, including lists and buttons:

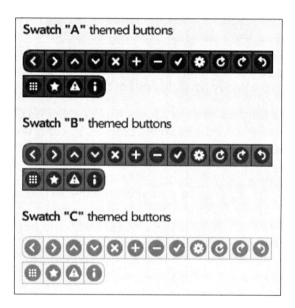

By default, if no theme is specified, jQuery Mobile assigns the "A" (black) swatch to headers and footers. Content blocks will default to "C" (light gray) swatch to maximize contrast. Any button that's placed in a bar is automatically assigned a swatch letter that matches its parent bar or content box: for example, "A" bars will have "A" buttons by default.

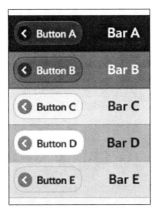

And if we ever get bored after combining and mixing and matching the swatches included in the default theme, jQuery Mobile allows for the creation of customized themes to help our own web application stand out.

Custom themes can modify a number of options, including shadows, icon sets, and corner radius values for buttons and boxes, as well as the more obvious foreground and background colors, gradients, and font family.

In order to apply a particular swatch to a page or specific element, we should make use of the `data-theme` attribute, which can be set to a letter from "a" to "z" and represents the swatch we want to be applied to the selected element.

> Note that the data-theme attribute can be applied to the whole page instead of just individual elements. So apply it to a `<div>` outside of the elements and it will cascade down to inner elements.

The following code might be a useful resource to better understand how we can apply different color swatches to elements on the same page:

```
<a href="#" data-role="button" data-theme="a">Button A</a>
<a href="#" data-role="button" data-theme="b">Button B</a>
<a href="#" data-role="button" data-theme="c">Button C</a>
<a href="#" data-role="button" data-theme="d">Button D</a>
<a href="#" data-role="button" data-theme="e">Button E</a>
```

The buttons created by the preceding code will look like the following image:

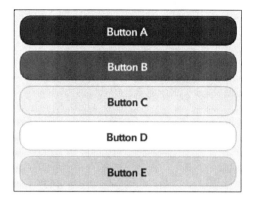

Summary

In this chapter, we have gone through an overview of what is jQuery Mobile and how its elements look and behave by default.

It is obvious that many of the aspects we have just mentioned will be discussed in greater detail in the following chapters, along with each covering technique, information, and general aspects of a specific element available for usage with the jQuery Mobile framework.

The basics for each jQuery Mobile-based application are pages, and, as such, in the next chapter, we will discover how we can create a simple page, set up more complex "multiple pages" layouts, and add dialogs and information boxes to the whole page.

4
Reading, Writing, Communicating: Content

Trying to communicate and provide information in an effective way can be a little trickier when we are targeting mobile devices; their screens are relatively small (ridiculously small if we think about our 24 inch iMac resting on our office desk), and we have already understood that we cannot display content in the way we used to, back in the days when desktop computers were the only way to access data on the Internet.

With the advent of mobile browsing, new solutions had to be found.

The jQuery Mobile framework provides a number of tools, widgets, and components which are extremely helpful in formatting our content and make it look elegant and put-together even on our beloved smaller-screen devices – well, especially for them!

In fact, the difficulty in designing, formatting, and correctly showing a page on a mobile device is going to become a no-brainer using the set of elements jQuery Mobile provides in order to allow for an easy styling of our web application content.

As for this chapter, we're going to cover:

- How content is displayed
- Using columns and grids
- A note on collapsible blocks
- Theming content

How content is displayed

Yes, there is nothing wrong in just writing down what our website or web application is about in the HTML file. It's always worked and always will.

The actual point here is taking advantage of the tools jQuery Mobile offers us to format our information, specifically for mobile devices.

For example, there are occasions in which the need for multiple columns may arise: we can use a layout grid, which is nothing more than some CSS-based columns.

Or, on a completely different note, we might just need to hide/show a block of content: collapsible blocks have been designed for this, and can be easily implemented in our site layout.

But before we begin analyzing any of the methods in which we are able to format our content according to our liking, we should take a look at how content is displayed in its basic HTML formatting.

Based upon the *"light hand approach"* (as they call it), jQuery Mobile lets the browser rendering take precedence over any other third-party styling, with exceptions made for the following little tweaks the framework applies to any page by default:

- Adding a bit of padding for a better readability
- Using the theming system to apply fonts and colors

This particular approach to styling by default should make the designers really happy, as they often find themselves fighting with preset colors schemes, default fonts, weird margin, and padding values and usually end up resetting everything and starting again from scratch.

Thankfully, the default padding value looks quite right and, as far as theming goes, we are able to easily customize (and create new) themes through CSS files and a theming framework which is extremely versatile and flexible.

Default HTML markup styling

So, what happens if we just write some HTML markup and want some text to be bold, emphasized, or hyper-linked? jQuery Mobile applies some basic styling to the elements and makes their look consistent with the simple and clean layout we have already seen in action.

The following screenshot represents how headings and standard paragraphs are displayed and generated by the following code:

```
<!DOCTYPE html>
<html>
<head>
  <title>Default HTML markup styling</title>

  <link rel="stylesheet" href="http://code.jquery.com/mobile/1.0a2/
jquery.mobile-1.0a2.min.css" />

  <script src="http://code.jquery.com/jquery-1.4.3.min.js"></script>
  <script src="http://code.jquery.com/mobile/1.0a2/jquery.mobile-
1.0a2.min.js"></script>
</head>

<body>
  <div data-role="page" id="home">
    <div data-role="content">
      <h1>H1 Heading</h1>
      <h2>H2 Heading</h2>
      <h3>H3 Heading</h3>
      <h4>H4 Heading</h4>
      <h5>H5 Heading</h5>
      <h6>H6 Heading</h6>

      <p>This is a paragraph. <strong>Lorem (bold)</strong> <em>ipsum
(emphasized)</em> <a href="#">dolor (link)</a> sit amet, consectetur
adipiscing elit.</p>

      <blockquote>Blockquote containing a <cite>cite</cite></
blockquote>

      <p>This is a paragraph. <strong>Lorem (bold)</strong> <em>ipsum
(emphasized)</em> <a href="#">dolor (link)</a> sit amet, consectetur
adipiscing elit.</p>
    </div>
  </div>
</body>
</html>
```

The result is shown in the following screenshot:

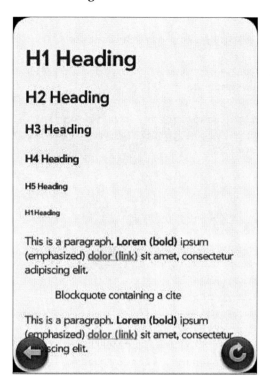

Similarly, the following code produces a preview of what lists and tables look like:

```
<!DOCTYPE html>
<html>
<head>
  <title>Default HTML markup styling</title>
  <link rel="stylesheet" href="http://code.jquery.com/mobile/1.0a2/
jquery.mobile-1.0a2.min.css" />
  <script src="http://code.jquery.com/jquery-1.4.3.min.js"></script>
  <script src="http://code.jquery.com/mobile/1.0a2/jquery.mobile-
1.0a2.min.js"></script>
</head>
<body>
  <div data-role="page" id="home">
    <div data-role="content">
      <ul>
        <li>Unordered list item 1</li>
        <li>Unordered list item 2</li>
        <li>Unordered list item 3</li>
      </ul>
```

```
    <ol>
      <li>Ordered list item 1</li>
      <li>Ordered list item 2</li>
      <li>Ordered list item 3</li>
    </ol>

    <table>
      <caption>Table caption</caption>

      <thead>
        <tr>
          <th scope="col">Name</th>
          <th scope="col">City</th>
          <th scope="col">Phone</th>
        </tr>
      </thead>

      <tfoot>
        <tr>
          <td colspan="5">Table foot</td>
        </tr>
      </tfoot>

      <tbody>
        <tr>
          <th scope="row">David Green</th>

          <td>New York City, NY</td>
          <td>555-0123</td>
        </tr>
        <tr>
          <th scope="row">Martha White</th>

          <td>Los Angels, CA</td>
          <td>555-0188</td>
        </tr>
        <tr>
          <th scope="row">Bobby Brown</th>

          <td>Washington, D.C.</td>
          <td>555-0110</td>
        </tr>
      </tbody>
    </table>
  </div>
 </div>
</body>
</html>
```

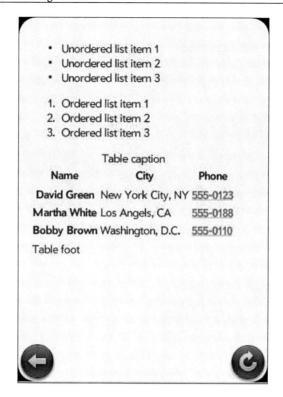

Using columns and grids

Even with no additional CSS code, jQuery Mobile formats our content in a simple, yet clean way. This also makes the text easier to read on mobile devices.

During the development of our web application, there might be times when we just need to place certain elements in a particular position, which would require a certain fluency in CSS (which we might not have).

Thankfully, jQuery Mobile provides a quick way to create a sort of grid layout: it applies a set of CSS rules with which we are able to obtain columns and rows to display our content as if it was in a table:

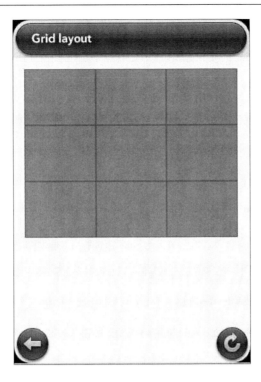

The page pictured above shows a 3x3 grid themed with Swatch B colors applied.

 The use of grids, though perfectly legitimate, is somewhat discouraged, due to the narrow screen width, which is a feature common to all the mobile devices.

In short:

- They are useful for displaying any sort of content which needs to be presented side-by-side (buttons and navigation bars are an example)
- They have no margins, no padding, no borders, and no background
- They, in general, do not interfere with any styling
- They are 100 percent wide
- They can have two, three, four, or five columns
- They can have multiple rows

How to create a simple grid with buttons

We'll begin by creating a simple grid with one row and two columns, each of which will contain a button:

1. In order to tell jQuery Mobile we want a two-column layout, we need to give a div the `ui-grid-a` class. This way, jQuery mobile will apply to the children divs (that is, our blocks or cells) the CSS rules necessary to take up 50 percent of the screen.

    ```
    <div class="ui-grid-a">
      <!-- blocks go here -->
    </div>
    ```

2. Depending on the number of columns we have specified, we are able to add our cells to the grid. For each cell, we need to specify the `ui-block-X` class, where X is a lowercase letter from a to z. The first block will be assigned the letter a, the second one will have a b, and so on:

    ```
    <div class="ui-grid-a">
      <div class="ui-block-a"></div>
      <div class="ui-block-b"></div>
    </div>
    ```

3. Next we add the buttons (one for each block), which is a fairly straightforward task:

    ```
    <div class="ui-grid-a">
      <div class="ui-block-a">
        <button type="submit">Click me!</button>
      </div>
      <div class="ui-block-b">
        <button type="submit">Clicky clicky</button>
      </div>
    </div>
    ```

4. We can obviously apply any theme we wish to the buttons, in order to make them stand out more or just as a style improvement:

```
<div class="ui-grid-a">
  <div class="ui-block-a">
    <button type="submit" data-theme="a">Click me!</button>
  </div>
  <div class="ui-block-b">
    <button type="submit" data-theme="b">Clicky clicky</button>
  </div>
</div>
```

Creating grids with more than two columns

The preset configuration layouts also comprehend grids with three, four, and five columns.

Needless to say, there is hardly any use at all for grids with four or five columns on devices that, by definition, have a small screen, but three-column layouts may come in handy sometimes.

Creating grids with multiple columns is no different from creating a simple two-column grid — we only need to change the class.

 We use letters from b to d to create grids with a number of columns from three to five.

In fact, jQuery Mobile has a set of CSS rules that make sure the grid always takes up the full width of the screen and all of the blocks have the same width too:

1. Our first step towards the realization of a four-column grid with two rows is creating a div element which has a `ui-grid-c` class:

```
<div class="ui-grid-c">
  <!-- we can have rows of four blocks in here! -->
</div>
```

2. As we have split the page up into four parts (25 percent wide each), we are able to fit four blocks for each row in the grid (letters from a through d):

```
<div class="ui-grid-c">
  <div class="ui-block-a">
    <p>First block, First row (A)</p>
  </div>
  <div class="ui-block-b">
    <p>Second block, First row (B)</p>
  </div>
  <div class="ui-block-c">
    <p>Third block, First row (C)</p>
  </div>
  <div class="ui-block-d">
    <p>Fourth block, First row (D)</p>
  </div>
</div>
```

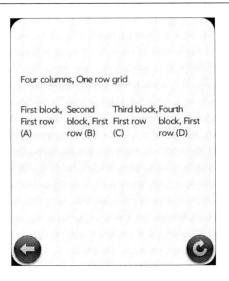

3. As for creating rows other than the first one, we just need to insert other blocks, repeating the letters we have already used. jQuery Mobile automatically recognizes our attempt at inserting a new row and breaks the line, so any time we add a block with the letter a, a new row is appended to the grid:

```
<div class="ui-grid-c">
  <div class="ui-block-a">
    <p>First block, First row (A)</p>
  </div>

  <div class="ui-block-b">
    <p>Second block, First row (B)</p>
  </div>

  <div class="ui-block-c">
    <p>Third block, First row (C)</p>
  </div>

  <div class="ui-block-d">
    <p>Fourth block, First row (D)</p>
  </div>

  <!-- second row -->
  <div class="ui-block-a">
    <p>First block, Second row (A)</p>
  </div>

  <div class="ui-block-b">
    <p>Second block, Second row (B)</p>
  </div>
```

```
<div class="ui-block-c">
  <p>Third block, Second row (C)</p>
</div>

<div class="ui-block-d">
  <p>Fourth block, Second row (D)</p>
</div>
</div>
```

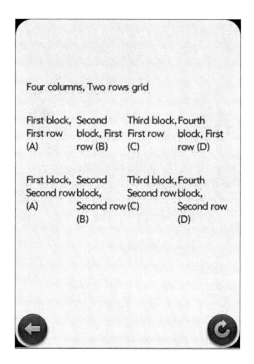

Using the same method, we can easily create grids with multiple columns and rows to easily align elements we absolutely need to display one next to another.

A note on collapsible blocks

On a completely different note, jQuery Mobile provides an easy-to-use and visually-appealing solution to hide and show content, namely, the so-called collapsible blocks.

Collapsible blocks should be already well-known to the web designers out there, and they have gained in popularity especially after the advent of JavaScript libraries and frameworks like jQuery, which have made writing the necessary code a matter of minutes to obtain a pane which shows its content once a button (or any kind of element, actually) is clicked. The following screenshot shows how jQuery Mobile renders, by default, any collapsible block we include into our web page:

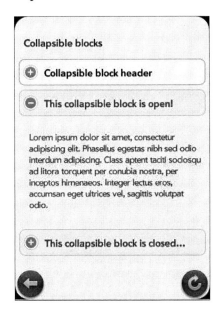

So, how do we create a (set of) collapsible block(s)?

1. Collapsible blocks are obtained by assigning a container the `data-role="collapsible"` attribute. As easy as that.

```
<div data-role="collapsible">
  <!-- this is a collapsible block -->
</div>
```

2. The jQuery Mobile framework needs a heading element to be present inside the container. The heading (which can be from h1 through h6) will be styled like a clickable button, and a plus (**+**) symbol will be added to its left to indicate it's expandable. Once we click the header/button and the content shows, a minus (**-**) symbol will replace the plus to indicate it's collapsible.

Where do I put the heading?

The heading can be placed anywhere inside the container. Remember that jQuery Mobile will use as a header the very first h-element it finds inside the container, and remove it from its original position.

Once the required header is provided, you can add any other h-element to the container and it will not be processed (that is, it will behave like a normal heading would).

```html
<div data-role="collapsible">
  <h3>Collapsible block header</h3>
  <p>Lorem ipsum dolor sit amet etc....</p>
</div>
```

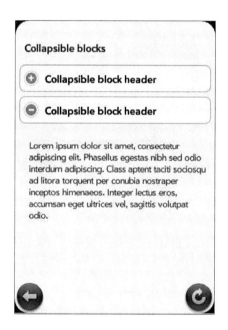

We used an h3 heading in this example, but any other heading would have looked just the same: jQuery Mobile changes completely the style of the heading to match a button's style.

3. We can specify whether we want a collapsible block to be expanded on page load or not by adding the `data-collapsed="true"` attribute to the container:

```html
<div data-role="collapsible" data-collapsed="true">
  <h3>This block will be collapsed (does not show content)</h3>
```

```
  <p>Lorem ipsum dolor sit amet etc....</p>
</div>

<div data-role="collapsible">
  <h3>This block will expand on page load</h3>
  <p>This text is visible right away!</p>
</div>
```

Nested collapsible blocks

Collapsible blocks can also be nested, resulting in a series of blocks which control various paragraphs and content:

1. To create a set of nested collapsible blocks, we only need to insert a block into another block, which will be its container:

    ```
    <!-- Top level collapsible block -->
    <div data-role="collapsible">
      <h3>Collapsible block header</h3>
      <p>Lorem ipsum dolor sit amet, consectetur adipiscing elit.</p>

      <!-- nested collapsible block -->
      <div data-role="collapsible">
        <h3>Nested collapsible block</h3>
        <p>Class aptent taciti sociosqu ad litora torquent per conubia
    nostra, per inceptos himenaeos.</p>
      </div>
    </div>
    ```

2. We may have any number of collapsible blocks nested; for example, here is another one:

    ```
    <!-- Top level collapsible block -->
    <div data-role="collapsible">
      <h3>Collapsible block header</h3>
      <p>Lorem ipsum dolor sit amet, consectetur adipiscing elit.</p>

      <!-- nested collapsible block -->
      <div data-role="collapsible">
        <h3>Nested collapsible block</h3>
        <p>Class aptent taciti sociosqu ad litora torquent per conubia
    nostra, per inceptos himenaeos.</p>

        <!-- nested into a nested block -->
        <div data-role="collapsible">
          <h3>Nested into a nested collapsible block</h3>
          <p>Integer lectus eros, accumsan eget ultrices vel, sagittis
    volutpat odio.</p>
    ```

```
      </div>
    </div>
  </div>
```

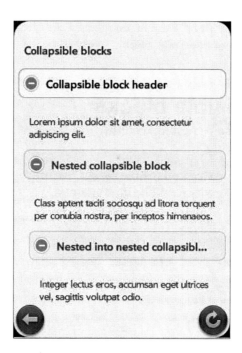

Collapsible sets

Collapsible sets are a certain number of collapsible blocks grouped together so that they act like an accordion widget: all other blocks close when a new one is opened:

1. A set of collapsible blocks is created by adding the `data-role="collapsible-set"` attribute to a container:

```
<div data-role="collapsible-set">
  <!-- collapsible blocks go here -->
</div>
```

2. We then add our collapsible blocks, as we would do in any other page:

```
<div data-role="collapsible-set">
  <div data-role="collapsible">
    <h3>Collapsible block in a set (1)</h3>
    <p>Lorem ipsum dolor sit amet, etc....</p>
  </div>

  <div data-role="collapsible">
```

```
  <h3>Collapsible block in a set (2)</h3>
  <p>Lorem ipsum dolor sit amet, etc....</p>
</div>

<div data-role="collapsible">
  <h3>Collapsible block in a set (3)</h3>
  <p>Lorem ipsum dolor sit amet, etc....</p>
</div>
```

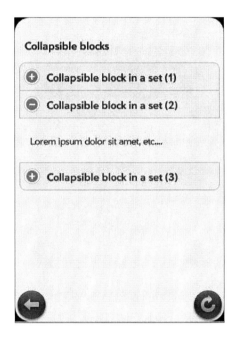

Nested collapsible blocks in collapsible sets

You cannot have nested collapsible blocks in a collapsible set, as jQuery Mobile treats all the collapsible blocks in the same way so that, when the nested collapsible block is clicked, all other blocks are closed and the content is hidden: even the container block is in fact closed, being part of the same collapsible set.

As of now, this problem seems to be fixed on certain handsets (Android 1.6 and 2.1 didn't even have this issue), but a bug is still filed for other devices.

Theming content

Theming content is extremely easy, thanks to the excellent theming system jQuery Mobile is shipped with.

As for collapsible blocks, we can add the `data-theme` attribute so we can choose from any swatch color. Various swatches appear as shown in the following screenshot:

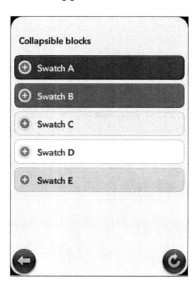

However, in order to have the content of collapsible blocks with the same color swatch, we need to add the same `data-theme` attribute to the outer container (in most cases, the page div).

A more interesting issue is the one related to the appearance of grids and their blocks: in order to obtain a grid of colorful cells, it is suggested to create an inner div which is styled using classes from a theme (swatch) of our liking:

```
<div class="ui-grid-b">
  <div class="ui-block-a">
    <div class="ui-bar ui-bar-b" style="height: 60px">
      <p>Content</p>
    </div>
  </div>
  <div class="ui-block-b">
    <div class="ui-bar ui-bar-b" style="height: 60px">
      <p>Content</p>
    </div>
  </div>
</div>
```

```
<div class="ui-block-c">
  <div class="ui-bar ui-bar-b" style="height: 60px">
    <p>Content</p>
  </div>
</div>
</div>
```

Of course, we could use the following code to wrap each block's content into the div we need once the page loads, and still get the same result with much less work to do!

```
<!-- in the HEAD -->
<script type="text/javascript">
  $(document).ready (function () {
    $('div[class^=ui-grid]').children ().each (function () {
      $(this).html ('<div class="ui-bar ui-bar-b" style="height:
60px">' + $(this).html () + '</div>');
    });
  });
</script>

<!-- in the BODY -->
<div data-role="page" id="home">
    <div data-role="content">
      <div class="ui-grid-b">
        <div class="ui-block-a"></div>
        <div class="ui-block-b"></div>
        <div class="ui-block-c"></div>

        <div class="ui-block-a"></div>
        <div class="ui-block-b"></div>
        <div class="ui-block-c"></div>

        <div class="ui-block-a"></div>
        <div class="ui-block-b"></div>
        <div class="ui-block-c"></div>
      </div>
    </div>
  </div>
<div>
```

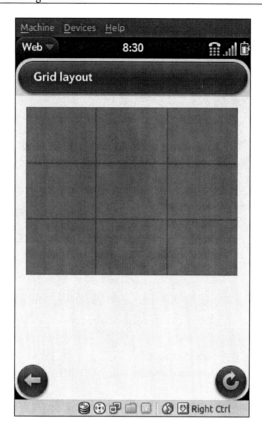

Summary

Dealing with content and displaying it on our page using jQuery Mobile is, as we've seen, fairly easy.

The problems we might run into when trying to accomplish a particular look and feel would be mainly related to the way jQuery Mobile processes the HTML markup and applies its own CSS rules to our elements.

However, the framework does its best not to interfere with our code and styling, preserving our layout as we thought it originally – there shouldn't be any problems then.

In the next chapter, we're going to see how to move between pages using toolbars, which can be customized to match our personal preferences, too!

5
Navigation Made Easier: Toolbars

One of the very first things we are used to looking for in the website is some form of navigation, a series of buttons or links we can use to move from one page to another.

There have been many studies on the field of how readers (or readers of a website) look at a page and process information, and how they gather the key words and sentences is quite a well-known fact as of now: people tend to look at the left-most content first and they place more attention on words and images which are bold and close to the top.

Website designers know this, and place the most important information near that area: the majority of the websites out there (exception made for those which are edgy and artistic – or try to) have their logo and menu on the top of the page. Some prefer a horizontal list of links; some go for vertical buttons.

In the mobile world, none of these key concepts change: jQuery Mobile provides a set of tools (well, toolbars) which can be used to deliver information (and links) to the user in a discreet, yet effective, manner.

Toolbars can be used as headers (usually containing the page title and some navigation buttons), footers (for navigation and informative purposes), and utility bars.

This chapter will address the following issues:

- How do toolbars actually work?
- Different types of bars
- On positioning
- Theming toolbars

How do toolbars actually work?

First of all, what exactly is a toolbar?

As the name quite clearly suggests, a toolbar is just a bar that contains buttons, text, or links we can interact with.

The following screenshot represents a standard page created with the aid of jQuery Mobile, in which a toolbar (header) is present:

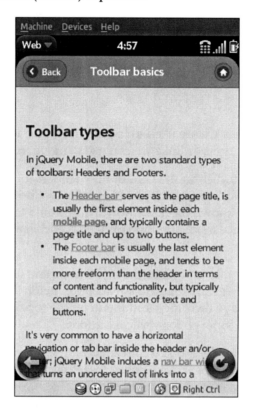

As we can see, the header has a different coloring than the rest of the page, in the attempt to make it stand out and be more noticeable.

On the bar we can find, from left to right, a button, some text in the center, and another button positioned far right.

The first button reads Back and it is obvious what would happen if we clicked it: jQuery Mobile would take us back to the previous page we were viewing.

The centered text is the page title, and is very helpful in reminding us what we are reading and/or where we are in the website.

Lastly, the circular button on the right is a link to the home page that is the site root. Clicking on this button will bring us back to the top-most directory.

Different types of bars

Being the great framework it is, jQuery Mobile provides a *standard set of bars and navigation tools to cover most standard scenarios*: header bars, footer bars, and navigation bars.

Header bars

The **Header bar** serves as the page title, is usually the first element inside each mobile page, and typically contains a page title and up to two buttons.

We can place buttons on the left or right of the page title element, which is a heading. All heading levels from H1 through H6 are allowed to represent the page title and are treated and styled the same, provided they are inside a div whose data-role is set to 'header'.

It's common practice to include a header element at the top of each page, though it is not required. Pages can also consist of the content portion exclusively.

Creating a header

Creating a header is really, really simple. Here's how:

1. Inside the page div, but before the content container, add a div with a data-role='header' attribute:

```
<div data-role="header">
  <!-- header content goes here -->
</div>
```

2. Inside the header container, add the heading for displaying the page title. Any heading level (H1-H6) can be used: the end result will be the same.

For consistency purposes, h1 headings seem to be preferred for header bars over any other lower-level heading.

```
<div data-role="header">
  <h1>Page title</h1>
</div>
```

The following screenshot shows our simple header bar:

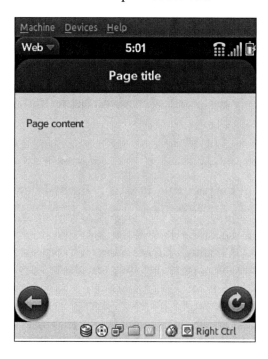

3. The framework automatically generates a back button and a home button on every page. To get rid of the back button, simply add the `data-backbtn="false"` attribute to the header container:

```
<div data-role="header" data-backbtn="false">
  <h1>Page title</h1>
</div>
```

Customizing buttons

By default, jQuery mobile creates slots of button on either side of the page title.

 If you're not happy with the default configuration, you can wrap your custom-styled markup into a div inside the header container: jQuery Mobile won't apply its styling to it.

- Buttons are anchor elements (or buttons created with button markup – see *Chapter 6, Mobile Clicking: Buttons*) which are as wide as the text they contain.
- The framework automatically sets the first link in the left button slot and the second link in the right.

We can use the data-icon attribute to add icons to the button.

```
<div data-role="header">
  <!-- This will appear on the left -->
  <a href="index.html" data-icon="arrow-l">Index</a>

  <h1>Page title</h1>

  <!-- This will appear on the right -->
  <a href="info.html" data-icon="plus">Add</a>
</div>
```

Because of our code, buttons appear on both sides of the heading:

- Buttons automatically adopt the color swatch of the header in which they are contained, but we can specify a data-theme attribute in order to change it:

```
<div data-role="header">
  <!-- This will appear on the left -->
  <a href="index.html" data-icon="arrow-l">Index</a>

  <h1>Page title</h1>
```

```
<!-- This will appear on the right (and is yellow) -->
<a href="info.html" data-icon="plus" data-theme="e">Add</a>
</div>
```

- A custom back button can be obtained by adding the `data-rel="back"` attribute to a button. The button will then behave as a back button would—go back one history entry and ignore the `href` attribute.

 We still provide a valid URL in the `href` attribute to make sure that our code works correctly on unsupported (Grade C) browsers too.

```
<div data-role="header">
  <!-- This goes back one history entry, regardless of the href
-->
  <a href="index.html" data-rel="back">Go back!</a>
  <h1>Page title</h1>
  <!-- This will appear on the right -->
  <a href="info.html" data-icon="plus">Add</a>
</div>
```

- In order to obtain a reverse transition without actually going back in history, we should use the `data-direction="reverse"` attribute instead of `data-rel="back"`:

```html
<div data-role="header">
  <!-- This causes a reverse transition, without actually going
back in history -->
  <a href="index.html" data-direction="reverse">Reverse!</a>

  <h1>Page title</h1>

  <!-- This will appear on the right -->
  <a href="info.html" data-icon="plus">Add</a>
</div>
```

- Buttons can be moved to the left or right, regardless of their position in the code. This applies also to a single button we want on the right.

> We can use classes that are also automatically applied by jQuery Mobile, in order to make sure a certain element has a specific set of characteristics.

```html
<div data-role="header">
  <a href="index.html" class="ui-btn-right">Right</a>
  <h1>Page title</h1>
  <a href="info.html" class="ui-btn-left">Left</a>
</div>
```

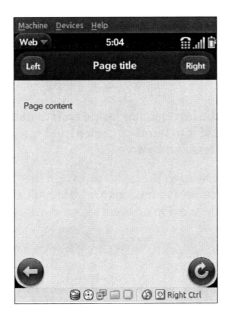

- The preceding code applies also to a single button we want on the right:

```
<div data-role="header">
  <a href="index.html" class="ui-btn-right">Right</a>
  <h1>Page title</h1>
</div>
```

Our button is now displayed on the right side of the header bar:

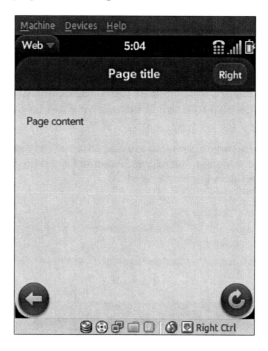

Footer bars

The **Footer bar** is usually the last element inside each mobile page, and tends to be more freeform than the header in terms of content and functionality, but typically contains a combination of text and buttons.

Footers have the same structure as the headers, except they are created by using the `data-role="footer"` attribute. No buttons are automatically added to the left or right side, nor is text, in case we don't provide it.

Creating a footer

The page footer is very similar to the header in terms of options and configuration:

1. Inside the page `div`, but after the content container, add a div with a `data-role="footer"` attribute:

```
<div data-role="footer">
  <!-- footer content goes here -->
</div>
```

2. Inside the footer container, add the heading for displaying the page title. Again, any heading level (H1-H6) can be used.

 Footer headings are best chosen in the h4-h6 range, in order to avoid any kind of compatibility issue on devices which don't support jQuery UI enhancements: the heading will then result in a standard heading smaller than the header's – because the footer is not as important as the heading.

```
<div data-role="footer">
  <h4>Page footer</h4>
</div>
```

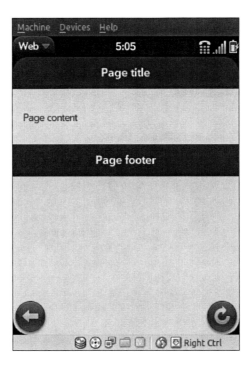

Adding buttons and other elements

By default, jQuery Mobile does not add any element to the footer to allow for more flexibility.

 Buttons are not placed left and right according to the page markup: instead they are positioned from left to right, in order of appearance in the code.

- Any link or valid button markup (or buttons created with button markup – see *Chapter 6, Mobile Clicking: Buttons*) will be automatically turned into a button.

- By default, there is no padding to accommodate elements in the footer. To include padding, add a `class="ui-bar"` to the footer container:

```
<div data-role="footer" class="ui-bar">
  <h4>Padded footer</h4>
</div>
```

- We can add buttons sitting in a row using the following code:

```
<div data-role="footer" class="ui-bar">
  <a href="left.html" data-icon="arrow-l" data-role="button">Left</a>
  <a href="up.html" data-icon="arrow-u"  data-role="button">Up</a>
  <a href="down.html" data-icon="arrow-d" data-role="button">Down</a>
  <a href="right.html" data-icon="arrow-r"  data-role="button">Right</a>
</div>
```

The buttons have some space in-between them:

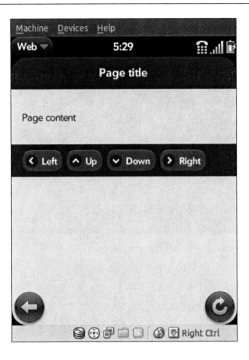

- We can group buttons together into a button set by wrapping them into a div with a `data-role="controlgroup"` attribute:

```
<div data-role="footer" class="ui-bar">
  <div data-role="controlgroup" data-type="horizontal">
    <a href="left.html" data-icon="arrow-l" data-
role="button">Left</a>
    <a href="up.html" data-icon="arrow-u"  data-role="button">Up</
a>
    <a href="down.html" data-icon="arrow-d" data-
role="button">Down</a>
    <a href="right.html" data-icon="arrow-r"  data-
role="button">Right</a>
  </div>
</div>
```

jQuery Mobile removed rounded corners of buttons, except for those at both ends of the group:

- Buttons can be assigned different color swatches specifying a data-theme attribute:

```
<div data-role="footer" class="ui-bar">
  <a href="left.html" data-icon="arrow-l" data-role="button" data-
theme="a">Left</a>
  <a href="up.html" data-icon="arrow-u"  data-role="button" data-
theme="b">Up</a>
  <a href="down.html" data-icon="arrow-d" data-role="button" data-
theme="c">Down</a>
  <a href="right.html" data-icon="arrow-r"  data-role="button"
data-theme="e">Right</a>
</div>
```

A sample of the four color swatches is represented in the following screenshot:

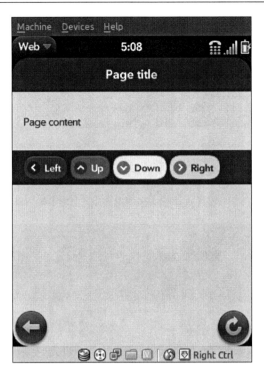

Navbars

"It's very common to have a horizontal navigation or tab bar inside the header and/or footer; jQuery Mobile includes a *navbar widget* that turns an unordered list of links into a horizontal button bar, which works well in these instances."

jQuery Mobile has a very basic navbar widget that is useful for providing up to five buttons with optional icons in a bar, typically within a header or footer.

Creating a navbar

1. A navbar is an unordered list of links wrapped into a container that has a `data-role="navbar"` attribute. We might want to place the navbar in the header (right after the page title) or in the footer:

```
<div data-role="footer">
  <div data-role="navbar">
    <!-- links go here -->
  </div>
</div>
```

2. We can then add the unordered list and two elements: the navbar items are set to divide the space evenly:

```
<div data-role="footer">
  <div data-role="navbar">
    <ul>
      <li><a href="one.html">One</a></li>
      <li><a href="two.html">Two</a></li>
    </ul>
  </div>
</div>
```

3. In this case, each button is half the width of the browser window:

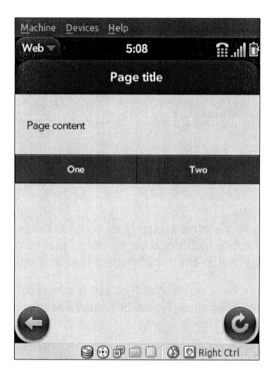

Customizing navbars

If we're not happy with the default configuration, we can tweak some of the settings to make our navbars look different:

- To set one of the links to the active state (that is, a selected link), simply add the class ui-btn-active to it:

```
<div data-role="footer">
```

```
<div data-role="navbar">
  <ul>
    <li><a href="one.html" class="ui-btn-active">One</a></li>
    <li><a href="two.html">Two</a></li>
  </ul>
</div>
</div>
```

The blue background indicates that a button is selected (active). Coloring (obviously) varies depending on the chosen theme:

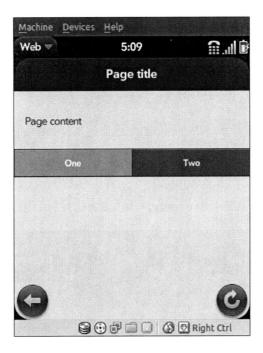

- If up to five elements are added, the space will be split evenly:

```
<div data-role="footer">
  <div data-role="navbar">
    <ul>
      <li><a href="one.html" class="ui-btn-active">One</a></li>
      <li><a href="two.html">Two</a></li>
      <li><a href="three.html">Three</a></li>
      <li><a href="four.html">Four</a></li>
      <li><a href="five.html">Five</a></li>
    </ul>
  </div>
</div>
```

The horizontal space is still split evenly, when the first button is selected:

If more than five elements are added, the *navbar* will wrap to multiple lines:

```
<div data-role="footer">
  <div data-role="navbar">
    <ul>
      <li><a href="one.html" class="ui-btn-active">One</a></li>
      <li><a href="two.html">Two</a></li>
      <li><a href="three.html">Three</a></li>
      <li><a href="four.html">Four</a></li>
      <li><a href="five.html">Five</a></li>
      <li><a href="six.html">Six</a></li>
    </ul>
  </div>
</div>
```

We can add any number of buttons. Just bear in mind the way in which jQuery Mobile handles a number of buttons greater than five:

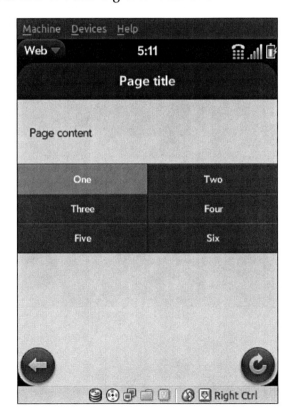

Icons can be added to navbar elements by specifying a data-icon attribute:

```
<div data-role="footer">
  <div data-role="navbar">
    <ul>
      <li><a href="one.html" data-icon="arrow-l" class="ui-btn-
active">One</a></li>
      <li><a href="two.html" data-icon="arrow-u">Two</a></li>
      <li><a href="three.html" data-icon="arrow-r">Three</a></li>
    </ul>
  </div>
</div>
```

Icons are displayed on top of the text by default:

On positioning

The jQuery Mobile framework provides three different ways in which we can position our bars, each of which proves useful in certain situations: fixed positioning (convenience of static toolbars without the drawbacks of implementing faux-scrolling); fullscreen positioning (toolbars hidden to maximize the viewport); and a persistent footer option.

Fixed positioning

We can apply fixed positioning to header or footer toolbars by adding a `data-position="fixed"` attribute to the element:

```
<div data-role="header" data-position="fixed">
  <h1>Fixed header</h1>
</div>
```

Fixed positioning lets the page content flow naturally, allowing us to take advantage of native scrolling instead of a scripting a faux-scrolling workaround. The header and footer divs are right in the flow of the document, but whenever they are out of view, you can tap the screen to make them appear. Tapping again or scrolling the page will cause them to reappear in the flow of the page (at the top and bottom).

The toolbars start in their natural positions on the page, but when a bar scrolls out of the viewport, the bar is automatically repositioned back into view.

At any time, tapping the screen will toggle the visibility of the fixed toolbars. Tapping the page when the toolbars aren't visible brings them into view; tapping again hides them until you tap again.

Fullscreen positioning

Fullscreen positioning is achieved by adding a `data-position="fixed"` attribute to the bar(s) we want to stay over the content. We also need to add a `data-fullscreen="true"` attribute to the page container we wish to be viewed fullscreen:

```
<div data-role="page" data-fullscreen="true">
  <div data-role="header" data-position="fixed">
    <h1>Fullscreen header</h1>
  </div>
  <!-- Content and footer containers follow -->
</div>
```

The fullscreen positioning is used "in special cases where you want the content to fill the whole screen, and you want the header and footer toolbars to appear and disappear when the page is clicked responsively — a common scenario for photo, image, or video viewers".

This is useful for applications like photo or video viewers where you want the content to fill the whole screen and toolbars are bound to appear by tapping the screen.

The toolbars in this mode will sit **over** page content, so not all content will be accessible with the toolbars open.

Persistent footer

By adding a footer with the same `data-id` attribute of another footer on another page, we can make use of the persistent footer feature and see the page content change while the footer remains fixed, even when transitioning to a new HTML page.

On page `one.html`:

```
<div data-role="footer" data-id="footer1">
  <div data-role="navbar">
    <ul>
      <li><a href="one.html" class="ui-btn-active">One</a></li>
      <li><a href="two.html">Two</a></li>
      <li><a href="three.html">three</a></li>
    </ul>
  </div>
</div>
```

On page `two.html`:

```
<div data-role="footer" data-id="footer1">
  <div data-role="navbar">
    <ul>
      <li><a href="one.html">One</a></li>
      <li><a href="two.html" class="ui-btn-active">Two</a></li>
      <li><a href="three.html">three</a></li>
    </ul>
  </div>
</div>
```

On page `three.html`:

```
<div data-role="footer" data-id="footer1">
  <div data-role="navbar">
    <ul>
      <li><a href="one.html">One</a></li>
      <li><a href="two.html">Two</a></li>
      <li><a href="three.html" class="ui-btn-active">three</a></li>
    </ul>
  </div>
</div>
```

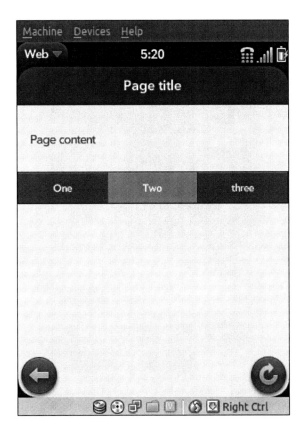

Theming toolbars

Both the header and footer bars will be styled by default with the theme's "a" color swatch because these bars are typically primary in the visual hierarchy of a page.

We can, of course, change the theme swatch to one of our liking by adding a `data-theme` attribute to the bar:

```
<div data-role="footer" data-theme="b">
  <h4>Swatch B</h4>
</div>
```

Buttons automatically inherit the color swatch from the bar they are contained in, but can be styled differently to increase contrast and visibility by adding a data-theme attribute.

The jQuery Mobile website has a demo of the variations that can be achieved by tweaking the theme swatches and buttons inside the headers and footers:

Summary

In this chapter, we have analyzed in great detail how and when to create and use toolbars in our mobile application: from providing information and navigation options (header), to linking to pages or different sections with footers and navbars.

In the next chapter, we will be dealing with buttons, whose markup will be extremely useful in creating and styling our custom button elements to be placed in toolbars of any kind. Many options and features (such as custom icons, effects, and coloring) will also be discussed.

6
Mobile Clicking: Buttons

What would the Internet be without buttons? No, seriously, every time we see a form, or there is the possibility to perform some sort of action, we instinctively look for a button to click in order to submit the information we wish to process.

The jQuery Mobile framework provides a series of options and markup facilities for us to choose from whenever we have to decide how to style the buttons we need in our mobile interface.

In fact, we might have trouble handling and creating buttons due to their nature: they are elements we can click, but we also expect them to (usually) do something other than navigate through the website.

However, jQuery Mobile makes heavy use of buttons as a means of navigation, often preferring buttons to regular links.

A simple example is the back button which is automatically added to most of the pages we create using the jQuery mobile framework; actually, though, this is a link which is styled as a button that links back to the previous page.

There is a fundamental difference between regular buttons and the so-called link buttons: the former are used in forms, and perform some kind of action; the latter can be used anywhere and are, in fact, mere means of navigation – exactly as an anchor link is.

In this chapter, we'll have a look at the following topics:

- What do buttons look and feel like in jQuery Mobile?
- Buttons markup and icons
- Displaying buttons
- Theming buttons

What do buttons look and feel like in jQuery mobile?

Each button we decide to create will be styled in the same way by the jQuery mobile framework, in order to improve the consistency of our web application.

But what exactly are buttons, and how do they look? First of all, we have a choice between link buttons and form buttons.

Link buttons are, actually, links which are styled as buttons. We can see an example of this type of button in almost all of our pages, in which the back button, placed on the top-left corner of the header bar, is a link to the previous page in the browsing history:

 For navigation purposes, you should use link buttons instead of regular buttons, which are best suited to submit form data because of the submit action they perform when clicked.

The jQuery Mobile framework automatically adds the necessary CSS classes to style the link as a button.

Here is an example of link buttons looking exactly like form buttons:

On the other hand, form buttons are "real" buttons, but are styled and behave just like link buttons.

Every time we need to create a form (see *Chapter 7, Transmitting Information: Forms*), we also need some input fields and at least one button to let the user submit the data they entered.

The following screenshot shows how a **Submit** button is displayed inside a form element:

The interesting thing about buttons is that jQuery Mobile actually keeps the original HTML-based button (created with the input tag) hidden and displays a custom button that looks better and behaves the same way; when we click on it, the event triggers another click event on the original, hidden button, which is responsible for actually submitting the form.

For example, the actual markup for a simple button would be as follows. Note that jQuery Mobile automatically applies a set of classes to modify the markup for a better user experience on mobile devices. The theme is also specified in the outer div, while the actual button element is replaced by a span element:

```
<div data-theme="c" class="ui-btn ui-btn-corner-all ui-shadow ui-btn-up-c">
  <span class="ui-btn-inner ui-btn-corner-all">
    <span class="ui-btn-text">Button element</span>
  </span>
  <button class="ui-btn-hidden">Button element</button>
</div>
```

Buttons markup and icons

There is, of course, only one way in which we are able to display a working button on a web page. However, there are a number of options we are allowed to apply to our buttons to further customize, change, or tweak their appearance and/or functioning.

Creating link buttons

These are the most straightforward buttons to create and place anywhere in a page.

Due to the nature of links though, they'd be better used exclusively for navigation purposes, whereas form buttons are better suited for, well, forms!

1. In the main content block of a page, we first need to have an anchor link element we want to turn into a button:

   ```
   <a href="somewhere.html">Click me!</a>
   ```

2. We can now add a `data-role="button"` attribute to the link: jQuery Mobile will do the rest and add the necessary styling to the link.

   ```
   <a href="somewhere.html" data-role="button">Click me!</a>
   ```

3. And that's it; we already have a button we can click to navigate through our website. Adding a `data-role="button"` attribute is enough to obtain the following screenshot:

Creating form buttons

As previously pointed out, jQuery Mobile automatically hides any button and displays a custom button, which will trigger any event on the original element.

In fact, the framework converts any button element or input with a type of button, submit, reset, or image into a link button; the link-based button is dynamically created by jQuery Mobile and behaves in the very same way as a regular link button would.

Form buttons are used to submit forms or interact with forms and are obtained in the same way as a regular HTML button is created – no additional options are required.

1. For example, here is how a button element is created. This line of code will be eventually substituted by a `div` and `span` element to which the necessary styling has been applied:

    ```
    <button>Button element</button>
    ```

2. In a very similar fashion, any input element with the type button, submit, reset, or image can be created this way. It will be assigned a class of `ui-btn-hidden` and a link-based button will be displayed instead:

    ```
    <input type="submit" value="Input element" />
    ```

The result can be seen in the following screenshot:

Adding icons

Buttons can have icons added in order to improve the graphical appearance of a web page.

The jQuery Mobile framework provides a set of icons most used in web applications. Icons are white in color and supplied in a sprite; to ensure good contrast on any background color, a semi-transparent black circle is added behind every icon (see the Appendix):

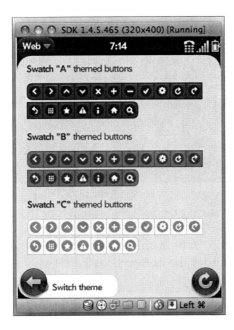

- To create a button with an icon, we need to add a data-icon attribute to the button markup:

  ```
  <a href="home.html" data-role="button" data-icon="home">Home
  page</a>
  ```

And we obtain a page similar to the following screenshot:

- By default, all icons are positioned on the left of the button text. We can change an icon position by specifying a `data-iconpos` attribute. Possible values are right, top, bottom, and they respectively place the icon on the right, above and under the button text:

```
<a href="home.html" data-role="button" data-icon="home" data-
iconpos="right">Home page</a>
```

Icons created using the preceding code are displayed in the following way:

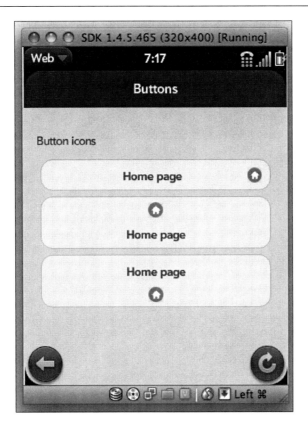

- The `data-iconpos` attribute can also have a value of `notext`: the button text will be hidden, leaving only the icon visible, and used as a title attribute.

```
<a href="home.html" data-role="button" data-icon="home" data-iconpos="notext">Home page</a>
```

A button icon is represented in a way similar to the following screenshot:

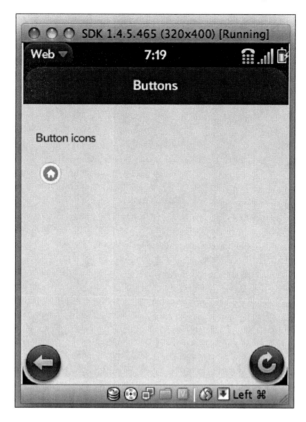

- For a list of all the available icons, see Appendix A. Using the icon name as the data-icon value will let you obtain a button adorned with the corresponding icon.

- Custom icons can be used with jQuery Mobile:

  1. We first need to specify a data-icon value that has a unique name such as `myapp-smile`:

     ```
     <a href="smile.html" data-role="button" data-icon="myapp-
     smile">Smile!</a>
     ```

  2. The jQuery Mobile framework will then create a new CSS class by prefixing `ui-icon-` to the `data-icon` value and apply it to the button. We will thus have a button with a `class="ui-icon-myapp-smile"`.

  3. In the stylesheet, we can then write a CSS rule that targets the `ui-icon-myapp-smile` class to specify the icon background source:

```
.ui .icon-myapp-smile {
  background-image: url('smile.png');
}
```

 To maintain visual consistency, the jQuery Mobile team suggests creating a white icon 18x18 pixels saved as a PNG-8 with alpha transparency.

Displaying buttons

We can go on customizing the look of our buttons well beyond just placing them on a page or just changing their icons or color. In fact, we can further tweak their appearance, relative to the page.

Inline buttons

By default, buttons take up the whole page width, as they are displayed as block-level elements.

We can, however, override the default settings and make buttons as wide as they need to be in order to correctly contain the button text. This is achieved by adding a `data-inline="true"` attribute to the button element:

```
<a href="inline.html" data-role="button" data-inline="true">Inline
button</a>
```

We can see the difference in the following screenshot:

In the case we have multiple buttons we wish to display inline, side-by-side, we can wrap them into a `div` element which has a `data-inline="true"` attribute.

This will cause the buttons to sit side-by-side on the same line, thanks to the container element which provides the inline attribute. If buttons are too large for one line, jQuery Mobile will split the elements on two (or more) lines:

```html
<div data-inline="true">
  <a href="open.html" data-role="button">Open</a>
  <a  href="close.html" data-role="button">Close</a>
  <a  href="save.html" data-role="button">Save</a>
</div>
```

The preceding code results in the following three buttons together on one line:

Using grids (see *Chapter 4, Reading, Writing, Communicating: Content*) we can also place buttons side-by-side, but taking up the full page width; this technique allows for two (up to five) normal full-width buttons to be placed on the same line:

```
<div class="ui-grid-a">
  <div class="ui-block-a">
     <a href="open.html" data-role="button">Open</a>
    </div>

  <div class="ui-block-b">
    <a href="close.html" data-role="button">Close</a>
  </div>
</div>
```

The code for inline buttons lets us create the following page:

Grouped buttons

Alternatively, in case we wish to visually group a set of buttons together to form a single block that looks like a navigation component, jQuery Mobile lets us make use of this feature which comes in handy in several situations.

Wrapping a set of buttons in a container with a `data-role="controlgroup"` attribute will cause the framework to create a vertical button group. This consists of a series of CSS rules that remove margins and shadows between the buttons.

```
<div data-role="controlgroup">
  <a href="index.html" data-role="button">Open</a>
  <a href="index.html" data-role="button">Close</a>
  <a href="index.html" data-role="button">Save</a>
</div>
```

Grouped buttons are displayed in the following way:

We can add a `data-type="horizontal"` attribute to the control group element in order to obtain a horizontal group of buttons. They are styled so that they float side-by-side; the width is large enough to contain all elements, but if too many elements are added – and they no longer fit the screen width – multiple rows will be used:

```
<div data-role="controlgroup" data-type="horizontal">
  <a href="index.html" data-role="button">Open</a>
  <a href="index.html" data-role="button">Close</a>
  <a href="index.html" data-role="button">Save</a>
</div>
```

Buttons grouped together can also be placed in line in order to create a "toolbar-like" feeling:

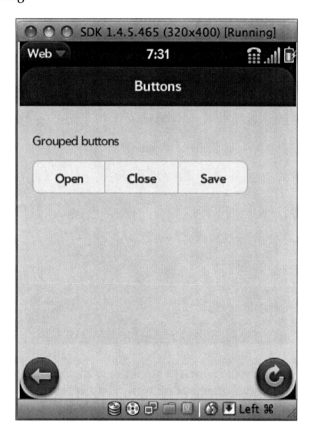

Theming buttons

Buttons can be styled in the very same way in which any other element is styled.

We can choose between the usual swatches (A, B, C, D, and E) and their combinations. In the jQuery Mobile documentation, we can find a couple of informative images that help in understanding how buttons, button icons, and text look when a certain theme is applied:

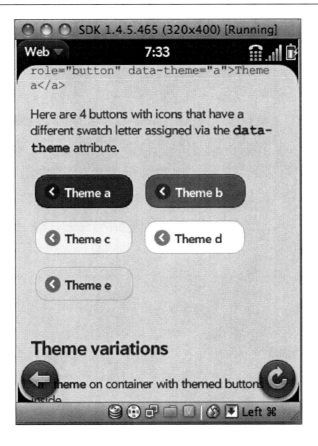

Summary

Buttons play an important role in several aspects of a web application: first of all, navigation. The jQuery mobile framework provides easy and quick ways in which we can turn our links into nice-looking buttons in order to eventually obtain a page and navigation system which look visually consistent.

It should be made clear, however, that buttons are extremely useful – and necessary – in other contexts too; for example, forms. Without buttons, we wouldn't be able to submit information and transmit data. A button needs to be easy to spot and use (that is, click), blending well with other elements in the page.

jQuery Mobile makes this button-form interaction as easy as possible, leaving unnecessary tasks out of the developer's responsibility. In the next chapter, we will see how.

7
Transmitting Information: Forms

If our goal is to create a static, dull website with no possible interaction from the user, we might as well skip this chapter. However, chances are that the majority of us are interested in learning how forms and various controls work and can be implemented using the jQuery Mobile framework.

Forms are particularly useful (well, necessary) whenever we need the user to submit any kind of data or information: submitting comments, posting a reply, taking a quiz, and purchasing something online – and generally, any action that counts on some interaction – are some of the activities forms are used for.

Along with forms, we will learn what elements we can create and make use of; jQuery Mobile provides a set of input elements which, acting on top of the standard HTML ones, offer a customized look and feel to match with the projects.

All of the elements are easy-to-use and of intuitive use, thanks to the simplicity in which sliders, select menus, input fields, and switches behave.

In this chapter, we'll go over the following topics:

- Form basics
- Text and password inputs, text areas, and search fields
- Flip switches, radio buttons, and checkboxes
- Sliders and select menus
- Theming forms

Form basics

First things first: all of the elements we might ever need in order to create a form (that is, inputs, buttons, switches, and so forth) are built by the jQuery Mobile framework on top of standard (native) HTML elements.

By creating a custom element, jQuery Mobile is thus able to provide a visually more appealing set of buttons and inputs to A-grade (and B-grade as well) mobile browsers. On lower-graded platforms (C-grade), no JavaScript or CSS is applied, and therefore plain HTML elements are used.

In a nutshell, jQuery Mobile applies its scripting to mobile devices which are known to support it and render the page correctly. Other browsers will fall back to a standard display as if jQuery Mobile was not used at all.

Form structure and initialization

Given the way in which the framework behaves, there are only a few differences we need to point out in order to create forms.

Basically, all forms should be constructed following the standard guidelines we would use in plain HTML: we still wrap all elements into a form tag and must decide whether we prefer to submit data via POST or GET.

Keep in mind jQuery is a JavaScript library, and as such, operates on the client-side. Unless we know what we're doing, we thus need to provide an action attribute which handles the data processing on the server-side.

The following code is a sample of the standard form structure we may employ (and modify) in our web pages:

```
<form action="form_process.php" method="POST" name="myform1"
id="myform1">
  <!-- elements go here -->
</form>
```

The form action attribute should be an existing page which is capable of processing the data we submit though the form.

> As jQuery Mobile makes use of a single-page navigation model (which allows for multiple pages to be present at the same time in the DOM) we must make sure all of our forms (and form elements as well) have a different form ID to prevent any kind of trouble.

If, for any reason, we'd like to prevent jQuery Mobile from enhancing any of our form elements, we can make sure some of them are not styled and present the standard HTML characteristics.

A simple, immediate way to accomplish this is by adding a `data-role="none"` attribute to the element(s) we wish to leave untouched, like so:

```
<input id="myinput1" data-role="none" value="" />
```

However, this may prove complicated or annoying if we prefer our markup to be as clean as possible or if we have a large number of elements we want to display with no enhancement whatsoever.

In the mobile initialization function, we can thus add the following line, which does the very same thing a `data-role="none"` does, but saves a lot of hassles in the majority of situations:

```
$(document).bind ('mobileinit',function () {
        $.mobile.page.prototype.options.keepNative = "textarea,
input#myinput";
});
```

We just list the elements we decided not to style and jQuery Mobile will not apply any kind of touch-friendly enhancement to them.

Input elements

The jQuery Mobile framework is designed so that all elements are flexible and comfortably fit the width of any mobile device screen; more importantly, depending on the screen width, jQuery Mobile displays labels and their associated elements side-by-side if the page is wider than 480px.

This means that, if our page is narrower than the above-mentioned size, elements will be placed under their label, to save horizontal space and improve the page layout.

On the other hand, on wider screens, labels and form elements are styled as inline (as opposed to the block styling applied in the other case) and take advantage of the greater width of the screen.

On a wider screen that allows side-by-side placement, we can further improve the overall look and feel by wrapping form elements and labels into a div or fieldset with a data-role="fieldcontain" attribute.

This makes sure the framework adds a thin vertical bottom border on this container to act as a field separator and visually aligns the label and form elements for quick scanning.

Text inputs

Text inputs (that is, actual text inputs, password inputs, and text areas) are the primary way in which we are able to enter information and interact with the form. These represent the free form element, as users are allowed to write nearly anything inside them unless we set (standard) HTML attributes to limit the field length or make use of some JavaScript to control the text entered.

Text fields

The only thing which is important to get right is to assign a unique ID to the input and the corresponding for attribute of the associated label. We then wrap all of it into a container which has a data-role="fieldcontain" attribute:

```
<div data-role="fieldcontain">
  <label for="myinput1">Text Input:</label>
  <input type="text" name="myinput1" id="myinput1" value="You can type
here!" />
</div>
```

The preceding code produces the following input field. Note the difference between styled and unstyled input fields:

Password fields

In order to display a password field, we specify a `type="password"` attribute, as we would in a standard HTML document. Obviously, any character which is entered is shown as a little circle to prevent anyone from reading our password over our shoulders.

Again, the markup isn't much different from what we've used in the text field example:

```
<div data-role="fieldcontain">
  <label for="mypwd1">Password Input:</label>
  <input type="password" name="mypwd1" id="mypwd1" value=""  />
</div>
```

The result can be seen in the following screenshot, together with an unstyled password field:

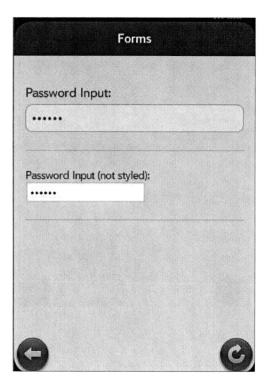

Text areas

Text area elements are used as multi-line text inputs.

The jQuery mobile framework prevents the use of a scrollbar by applying an auto-grow feature to text area elements: their height will then auto-grow to a suitable size as you write!

The following code produces a sample text area element:

```
<div data-role="fieldcontain">
  <label for="mytextarea1">Textarea:</label>
  <textarea cols="20" rows="10" name="mytextarea1" id="mytextarea1">
    Write here and see it auto-grow!
  </textarea>
</div>
```

Text areas (styled and unstyled) are displayed like this:

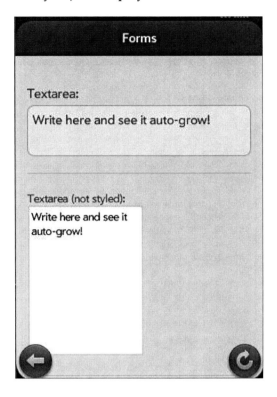

Search inputs

Search inputs share with other text inputs all of the characteristics of input elements, but jQuery Mobile further enhances text inputs by adding a magnifier icon on the left and, once something is written in them, an X icon to clear the field on the right.

We can create search inputs by specifying a `type="search"` attribute in any input element:

```
<div data-role="fieldcontain">
  <label for="mysearchinput1">Search Input:</label>
  <input type="search" name="mysearchinput1" id="mysearchinput1"
value="" />
</div>
```

Search inputs are displayed like this. Notice how different they look thanks to the enhancements by jQuery Mobile:

Flip switches, radio buttons, and checkboxes

Whenever we need the user to choose between a restricted set of answers or options, it's usually a good idea not to make them write into a text field: people are funny beings and often "mistakenly" enter some completely unrelated (though sometimes hilarious) text into a field we might value as important.

For this reason, we might force the user to answer either "Yes" or "No" to a yes/no question, or choose one (or more) option(s) out of a number of possibilities.

Flip toggle switches

Binary flip toggle switches are UI elements used for any binary (yes/no, on/off, left/right, and so on) type of data input.

Actually, flip toggles are a particular type of select menu: the first option is styled as the "off" state of the switch, whereas the second option corresponds to the "on" state of the switch.

It is not possible to add a third option, as jQuery Mobile doesn't know how to handle it and the whole behavior of the flip toggle would be compromised.

To create a flip toggle, we can add a `data-role="slider"` attribute to a select menu.

 Note that if we don't provide any data-role attribute, jQuery Mobile will treat the flip toggle switch as a select menu and all the enhancements applied to it will be those of the select menus.

In order to prevent jQuery Mobile from styling a flip toggle, we need to provide a `data-role="none"` attribute, but the element will be displayed as a non-styled select menu – there is no such element (on/off switch) in plain HTML!

The following code creates a flip toggle switch:

```
<div data-role="fieldcontain">
  <label for="mytoggle1">Flip toggle:</label>
  <select name="mytoggle1" id="mytoggle1" data-role="slider">
    <option value="off">Off</option>
    <option value="on">On</option>
  </select>
</div>
```

The following screenshot shows how flip toggles are displayed based on `data-role`:

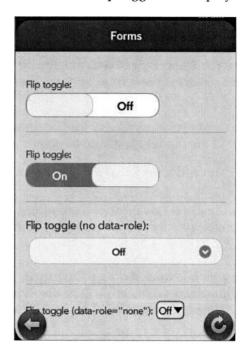

Radio buttons

Radio buttons are UI elements which come in handy when we want the user to select one item from a list of several options.

They are usually displayed as a circular hole containing a white space (unselected) or a dot (selected), with an adjacent text (a label) describing the option.

The jQuery Mobile framework enhances radio buttons by providing a more user (and touch)-friendly component which is presented in a button-like fashion.

Radio buttons can be grouped in sets of two or more using a `fieldset` with a `data-role="controlgroup"`: jQuery Mobile will automatically remove margins and borders from the buttons, and users can select only one of the radio buttons grouped this way.

The legend element of the `fieldset` will serve as a label for the radio buttons group:

- We still make use of the container div with a `data-role="fieldcontain"` to separate the radio buttons from other elements on the page:

  ```
  <div data-role="fieldcontain">
  ```

```
  <!-- fieldset goes here -->
</div>
```

- We then add a `fieldset` with a `data-role="controlgroup"` attribute to group radio buttons together:

```
<div data-role="fieldcontain">
  <fieldset data-role="controlgroup">
    <legend>Please make a choice:</legend>

    <!-- radio buttons go here -->
  </fieldset>
</div>
```

- Radio buttons can now be added. We can also specify which one will be selected by default on page load:

```
<div data-role="fieldcontain">
  <fieldset data-role="controlgroup">
    <legend>Please make a choice:</legend>
    <input type="radio" name="myradio1" id="myradio1"
value="radio1" />
    <label for="myradio1">First</label>
    <input type="radio" name="myradio2" id="myradio2"
value="radio2" checked="true" />
    <label for="myradio2">Second</label>
    <input type="radio" name="myradio3" id="myradio3"
value="radio3" />
    <label for="myradio3">Third</label>
  </fieldset>
</div>
```

- Vertical radio buttons are displayed as shown in the following screenshot. Standard radio buttons can also be created.

- We can also group radio buttons horizontally – so that they are displayed side-by-side – by adding a `data-type="horizontal"` attribute to the fieldset:

```
<div data-role="fieldcontain">
  <fieldset data-role="controlgroup" data-type="horizontal">
    <legend>Please make a choice:</legend>

    <input type="radio" name="myradio1" id="myradio1"
value="radio1" />
    <label for="myradio1">First</label>

    <input type="radio" name="myradio2" id="myradio2"
value="radio2" checked="true" />
    <label for="myradio2">Second</label>

    <input type="radio" name="myradio3" id="myradio3"
value="radio3" />
    <label for="myradio3">Third</label>
  </fieldset>
</div>
```

- Using jQuery Mobile, we can make a choice of displaying radio buttons in a variety of ways, whereas unstyled (standard) radio buttons always look the same:

Checkboxes

Checkboxes are UI elements used to provide a list of options, of which more than one can be selected.

They can be grouped together (much like radio buttons) horizontally or vertically, or can be used singularly to let the user (dis)agree with a statement:

1. To create a checkbox, simply add a `type="checkbox"` attribute to an input element:

```
<div data-role="fieldcontain">
  <fieldset data-role="controlgroup">
    <legend>Do you agree?</legend>

    <input type="checkbox" name="mycb1" id="mycb1" />
    <label for="mycb1">Yes, I agree!</label>
```

```
      </fieldset>
    </div>
```

2. Notice that styled checkboxes provide a more user-friendly interface than unstyled elements:

3. We can also group any number of checkboxes vertically, so as to give the user a choice between them:

```
<div data-role="fieldcontain">
  <fieldset data-role="controlgroup">
    <legend>What are your favorite colors?</legend>

    <input type="checkbox" name="mycb" id="mycb1" />
    <label for="mycb1">Black</label>

    <input type="checkbox" name="mycb" id="mycb2" />
    <label for="mycb2">Grey</label>

    <input type="checkbox" name="mycb" id="mycb3" />
    <label for="mycb3">White</label>
  </fieldset>
</div>
```

4. We can group checkboxes as we would do with radio buttons:

5. Eventually, we can even display a group of checkboxes horizontally by adding a `data-type="horizontal"` to the `fieldset`; and as the boxes are hidden, they pretty much look like buttons:

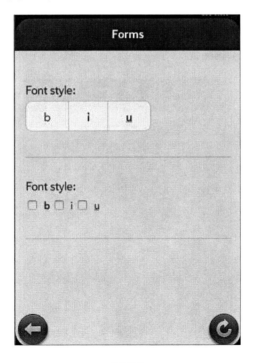

Sliders and select menus

At last, we're going to see how sliders and the select menu work and how they can be modified to suit our needs.

These are two of the most versatile elements we can include in a form, due to their flexible nature; we can use sliders to select a value from a range of numbers, and select menus are traditionally used to select shipping methods or some similar kind of information.

Sliders

Slider elements have been introduced recently by the HTML5 standard and are a particular UI element that, once you have specified the minimum and maximum values, lets the user choose one of those values in-between.

To create a slider, add a `type="range"` attribute to an input element.

We then specify the min and max attributes, as well as the value attribute, which represent the position the track handle starts in:

```
<div data-role="fieldcontain">
        <label for="slider">Input slider:</label>
        <input type="range" name="myslider1" id="myslider1" value="50"
min="0" max="100"  />
</div>
```

Sliders are displayed like this:

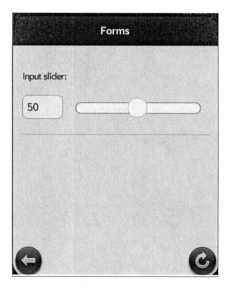

Select menus

The basics of the select menu is that, when a select menu is inactive, it displays a single value; when a click event is registered on it, the menu drops down a list of options we can choose from.

To create a select menu, we do exactly as we would in plain HTML:

```
<div data-role="fieldcontain">
  <label for="myselect1" class="select">Choose one:</label>
  <select name="myselect1" id="myselect1">
    <option value="option1">Option 1</option>
    <option value="option2">Option 2</option>
    <option value="option3">Option 3</option>
  </select>
</div>
```

A select menu is shown in the following screenshot, next to an unstyled element:

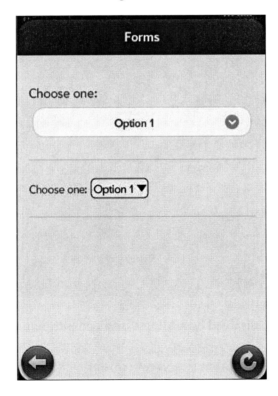

- We can add a placeholder element to the select menu so that it is visible by default (but hidden by jQuery Mobile once the drop-down list opens). A valid option, as per jQuery Mobile, must have both text and value; if one of the two is missing, the option will be treated as a placeholder. Alternatively, we can add a `data-placeholder="true"` attribute to an option:

```
<div data-role="fieldcontain">
  <label for="myselect1" class="select">Choose one:</label>
  <select name="myselect1" id="myselect1">
    <option>Please choose</option>

    <option value="option1">Option 1</option>
    <option value="option2">Option 2</option>
    <option value="option3">Option 3</option>
  </select>
</div>
```

The **Please choose** option (in our example) is automatically recognized as a placeholder and shown accordingly by jQuery Mobile:

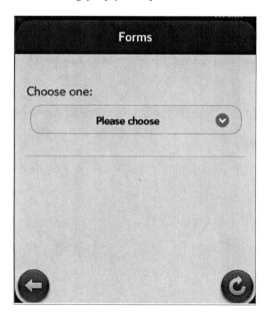

- Options can be disabled by adding a disabled attribute to the option tag:

```
<div data-role="fieldcontain">
  <label for="myselect1" class="select">Choose one:</label>
  <select name="myselect1" id="myselect1">
    <option>Please choose</option>

    <option value="option1" disabled="true">Option 1</option>
    <option value="option2">Option 2</option>
```

```
      <option value="option3">Option 3</option>
   </select>
</div>
```

- If a select menu contains the `optgroup` elements, jQuery Mobile divides options and groups them based on their label attribute's text:

```
<div data-role="fieldcontain">
   <label for="myselect1" class="select">Choose one:</label>
   <select name="myselect1" id="myselect1">
      <option>Please choose</option>
      <optgroup label="Group 1">
         <option value="option1" disabled="true">Option 1</option>
         <option value="option2">Option 2</option>
         <option value="option3">Option 3</option>
      </optgroup>
      <optgroup label="Group 2">
         <option value="option1">Option 1</option>
         <option value="option2">Option 2</option>
         <option value="option3">Option 3</option>
      </optgroup>
   </select>
</div>
```

- A group of items is shown in the following screenshot:

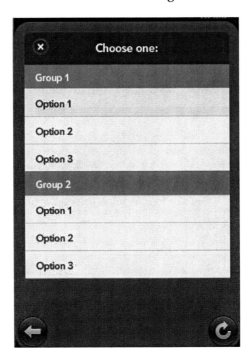

- We can also create select menus so that multiple options can be selected by adding multiple attributes to the markup. If this is the case, jQuery Mobile automatically creates a header element inside the menu which provides the way to close the drop-down list, as clicking an element inside the widget will not close it. Once more than two elements are selected, a counter element will appear on the right side of the button.

```
<div data-role="fieldcontain">
  <label for="myselect1" class="select">Choose one:</label>

  <select name="myselect1" id="myselect1" multiple="true">
    <option>Please choose</option>

    <optgroup label="Group 1">
      <option value="option1" disabled="true">Option 1</option>
      <option value="option2">Option 2</option>
      <option value="option3">Option 3</option>
    </optgroup>

    <optgroup label="Group 2">
      <option value="option1">Option 1</option>
      <option value="option2">Option 2</option>
      <option value="option3">Option 3</option>
    </optgroup>
  </select>
</div>
```

The selected items are listed once the select menu is closed and a number is added as a counter:

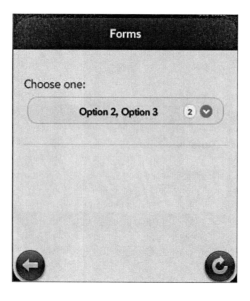

Theming forms

Pretty much like any other element, form elements can be styled by applying different swatches to their markup.

Colors will automatically change so that they are consistent with other elements in the page. We can see an example of how color contrast and coordination is changed when applying, for example, a Swatch B:

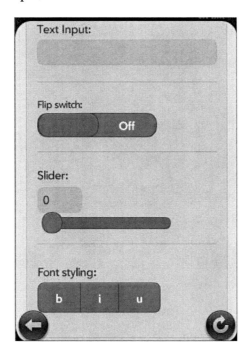

Also, the yellow-based theme may seem a little too much, but color contrast is handled very well and everything can be read easily:

Summary

This chapter has taken a tour of the most important features of forms and has demonstrated how easily we can play around with the custom elements jQuery Mobile provides us with and make them suit our needs with very little effort.

We're almost close to the end, but the next chapter, the last one, will take care of explaining what list views are and how they can be used to display and group information, images, and any other kind of content.

8
Organizing Information: List Views

You might have noticed that the vast majority of websites built using jQuery Mobile have their content laid out in very similar ways; sure, they differ in the design, colors, and overall feel, but they all have a list-based layout.

There is a way in which we can organize our information and take advantage of each and every space in the browser: information is displayed vertically, one piece under another. There are no sidebars of any kind and links are organized in lists – for a cleaner and tidy look.

But list views are also used to actually be a list of information. Some examples may be lists of albums, names, tasks, and so on: after all, our purpose is to build a mobile web application and the majority of services and pages can be organized in a way which closely resembles a list.

The jQuery Mobile framework obviously makes available a set of list types, each of which is best suited to certain situations and applications: we can have numbered lists, nested lists, lists with icons, thumbnails, and many other improvements, and user-friendly options that will no doubt enhance the usability of our list view elements.

This chapter will address the following issues:

- Basics and conventions for list views
- Choosing the list type, as per your requirements

Basics and conventions for list views

Due to the particular nature of lists, list views are coded exactly the same way a standard HTML unordered list would.

After all, the purpose of list views is to organize our information in a tidy way, presenting a series of links which are placed one under another; the easiest way to grasp their usefulness is, in my opinion, imagining a music player application.

A music player would need a clean enough interface, listing the artists, albums, and songs by name. In order to play a song, the user would need to select an artist, and then choose the album in which the song he wishes to play has been released.

To create our first view (artists), we would use the following code. Make sure you add the `data-role="listview"` attribute to the unordered list tag:

```
<ul data-role="listview">
  <li><a href="astra.html">Astra</a></li>
  <li><a href="zappa.html">Frank Zappa</a></li>
  <li><a href="tull.html">Jethro Tull</a></li>
  <li><a href="radiohead.html">Radiohead</a></li>
  <li><a href="who.html">The Who</a></li>
</ul>
```

The jQuery Mobile framework automatically styles the list elements accordingly, and adds a right arrow icon. List elements fill the full width of the browser window:

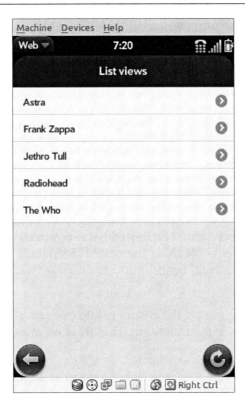

Whenever an item is selected (click/tap event), jQuery Mobile will parse the code inside the list element and issue an AJAX request for the first URL found.

The page (obtained via AJAX) is then inserted into the existing DOM and a page transition event is triggered.

 The default page transition is a slide-left animation; clicking the back button on the newly displayed page will result in a slide-right animation.

Choosing the list type as per your requirements

A somewhat large variety of lists are available for us to choose from in order to make use of the type of list view that is best suited to our needs.

Below are listed (sorry, no pun intended!) the different types of list views along with a brief description of how to use them and what part of code we need to change in order to obtain a certain list view.

Nested lists

Bearing in mind that list views elements are based on the standard HTML unordered list element, we might be wondering what would happen if we try and create a second list inside a list view.

By nesting a `ul` element inside list items, jQuery Mobile will adopt a different kind of behavior to our list items.

Our first step toward the creation of a nested list is removing any link present in the list item, as a click event will show the nested list instead of redirecting to another page. The child list will be put into a new "page" with the title of the parent in the header.

We're now implementing nested list elements into our sample music player interface by changing our markup to the following. This way, we are able to browse artists and albums.

Please note that we have removed any links to external pages:

```
<ul data-role="listview">
  <li>Astra
    <ul>
      <li><a href="astra_weirding.html">The Weirding</a></li>
    </ul>
  </li>
  <li>Frank Zappa
    <ul>
      <li><a href="zappa_hotrats.html">Hot Rats</a></li>
      <li><a href="zappa_yellowshark.html">Yellow Shark</a></li>
    </ul>
  </li>
  <li>Jethro Tull
    <ul>
      <li><a href="tull_aqualung.html">Aqualung</a></li>
      <li><a href="tull_thick.html">Thick as a Brick</a></li>
    </ul>
  </li>
  <li>Radiohead
    <ul>
```

```
    <li><a href="radiohead_ok.html">OK Computer</a></li>
    <li><a href="radiohead_rainbows.html">In Rainbows</a></li>
    <li><a href="radiohead_kol.html">The King of Limbs</a></li>
  </ul>
</li>
<li>The Who
  <ul>
    <li><a href="who_next.html">Who's Next</a></li>
    <li><a href="who_q.html">Quadrophenia</a></li>
    <li><a href="who_tommy.html">Tommy</a></li>
  </ul>
</li>
</ul>
```

If we clicked on the `Radiohead` element, we would then be able to see the following page:

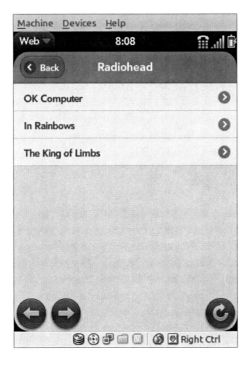

 By default, child list will be given a Swatch B theme to indicate they are at a secondary level of navigation; we can select a different color swatch by specifying a data-theme attribute on the child list element.

We can see the header turned blue, and the artist name is used as the header. We have a choice to go back to the previous page (artists) or click again onto a list item (album) to view more.

Numbered lists

Our music player interface has reached the point in which we need to list the tracks contained in an album. Of course, tracks have a sequence, and we want to give the user the possibility to see what track number is without having to count them all – and without writing numbers manually, that would be terrible!

In a very similar fashion, we can use ordered list elements (ol) to obtain numbering: jQuery Mobile will try to use CSS to display numbers or, if not supported, JavaScript.

The following code lists all of the tracks for an album:

 There is no limit to the number of lists you can nest.

```
<ul>
<!-- … -->
<li>Radiohead
  <ul>
    <li><a href="radiohead_ok.html">OK Computer</a></li>
    <li><a href="radiohead_rainbows.html">In Rainbows</a></li>
    <li>The King of Limbs
      <ol>
        <li><a href="play.html">Bloom</a></li>
        <li><a href="play.html">Morning Mr. Magpie</a></li>
        <li><a href="play.html">Little by Little</a></li>
        <li><a href="play.html">Feral</a></li>
        <li><a href="play.html">Lotus Flower</a></li>
        <li><a href="play.html">Codex</a></li>
        <li><a href="play.html">Give Up the Ghost</a></li>
        <li><a href="play.html">Separator</a></li>
      </ol>
    </li>
  </ul>
</li>
<!-- … -->
</ul>
```

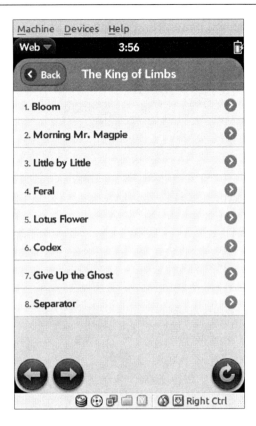

Read-only lists

Sometimes, we just need to list a certain number of items and don't want to provide a link for them.

Read-only lists can be created by omitting the anchor link element. The jQuery mobile framework will automatically style the list items so that they look flat. They are displayed using a Swatch C coloring.

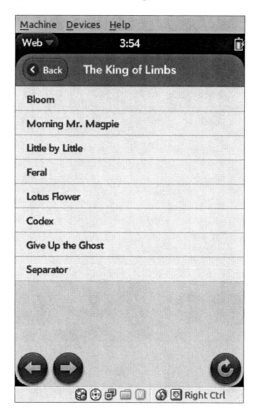

However, this kind of list is usually displayed using a `data-inset="true"` to the (un)ordered list attribute, which inserts some spacing and allows lists that have borders, or don't take up the whole page, to coexist with other elements on the page.

```
<li>The King of Limbs
  <ol data-inset="true">
    <!-- list items with no anchor links -->
  </ol>
</li>
```

We can see how a list with the `data-inset` attribute looks in the following screenshot:

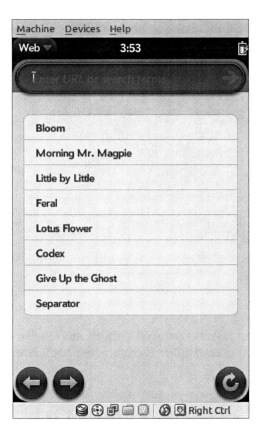

Split button lists

There may be cases in which we wish to be able to let the user perform more than one action on the same list item. For example, were the user browsing a list of albums, they should be presented with the possibility to buy, rate, or listen to each of them in a quick and simple way.

In order to provide such functionality, a split button can be used to offer two (or more) clickable items for each list item.

To create a split list item, simply add a second link to the list item; jQuery Mobile will then add a vertical line to separate the two buttons.

If we were to implement a "buy album" button next to the album name, we would need the following code:

```
<ul data-role="listview">
  <!-- … -->
  <li>Radiohead
    <ul>
      <li>
        <a href="radiohead_ok.html">OK Computer</a>
        <a href="purchase.html">Buy album</a>
      </li>
      <li>
        <a href="radiohead_rainbows.html">In Rainbows</a>
        <a href="purchase.html">Buy album</a>
      </li>
      <li>
        <a href="radiohead_kol.html">The King of Limbs</a>
        <a href="purchase.html">Buy album</a>
      </li>
    </ul>
  </li>
  <!-- … -->
</ul>
```

The following screenshot shows how split buttons are rendered by jQuery Mobile. Notice the thin vertical line separating the main text body from the arrow button on the right:

jQuery Mobile sets the title attribute of the second button to the text of the anchor link. You may want to use some descriptive text.

The icon can be changed by specifying a `data-split-icon` attribute with the icon name we wish to display:

```
<ul data-role="listview">
  <!-- … -->
  <li>Radiohead
    <ul data-split-icon="gear">
      <li>
        <a href="radiohead_ok.html">OK Computer</a>
        <a href="purchase.html">Buy album</a>
      </li>
      <li>
        <a href="radiohead_rainbows.html">In Rainbows</a>
        <a href="purchase.html">Buy album</a>
      </li>
      <li>
        <a href="radiohead_kol.html">The King of Limbs</a>
        <a href="purchase.html">Buy album</a>
      </li>
    </ul>
  </li>
  <!-- … -->
</ul>
```

In the following screenshot, the arrow icon has been replaced with a gear icon:

Spicing up your lists

Sure, list views appear to be of undoubted usefulness already, but there are some details and tweaks that will make them even more interesting and fun to use and work with.

Count bubbles

To proceed with our music player interface example, we are about to show the number of tracks in each album into a count bubble.

Count bubbles are count indicators sitting on the right of the list item, and they are of proven usefulness in many e-mail applications as indicators of how many messages are contained in a certain folder.

To create a count bubble, we simply wrap the number in an element with a class of `ui-li-count`, just like the following:

```
<ul data-role="listview">
  <!-- … -->
  <li>Radiohead
```

```
<ul data-list-icon="gear">
  <li>
    <a href="radiohead_ok.html">OK Computer</a>
    <a href="purchase.html">Buy album</a>
    <span class="ui-li-count">12</span>
  </li>
  <li>
    <a href="radiohead_rainbows.html">In Rainbows</a>
    <a href="purchase.html">Buy album</a>
    <span class="ui-li-count">10</span>
  </li>
  <li>
    <a href="radiohead_kol.html">The King of Limbs</a>
    <a href="purchase.html">Buy album</a>
    <span class="ui-li-count">8</span>
  </li>
</ul>
  </li>
  <!-- … -->
</ul>
```

Clicking on count bubbles does not trigger any event.

List dividers

To allow for an easier browsing experience, we might want to add headers for each letter in the "artists" view. The user will be able to identify their favorite band looking after the right letter.

The jQuery Mobile framework supports turning a list item into a list divider by adding a `data-role="list-divider"` attribute to any list item:

```
<ul data-role="listview">
  <li data-role="list-divider">A</li>
  <li><a href="astra.html">Astra</a></li>

  <li data-role="list-divider">F</li>
  <li><a href="zappa.html">Frank Zappa</a></li>

  <li data-role="list-divider">J</li>
  <li><a href="tull.html">Jethro Tull</a></li>

  <li data-role="list-divider">R</li>
  <li><a href="radiohead.html">Radiohead</a></li>

  <li data-role="list-divider">W</li>
  <li><a href="who.html">The Who</a></li>
</ul>
```

As you can see, artists are now grouped by letter.

List dividers are styled using a Swatch B, by default; this can be changed by specifying a `data-group-theme` attribute.

Images

Album artwork can be added to the list item by providing an image as the first child of the list item; that is, the `img` tag must be before any link or text we want to be displayed in the list item.

The jQuery Mobile framework will automatically resize the image to an 80 pixels square.

> Note, however, that if an image is larger than 80x80 pixels, it will still need the bandwidth to travel from the server to the client (that is, your computer). In addition, images that are not square in proportion will not look right when resized.

```
<ul data-role="listview">
  <!-- … -->

  <li>Radiohead
    <ul data-list-icon="gear">
      <li>
        <img src="ro_artwork.png" />
        <a href="radiohead_ok.html">OK Computer</a>
        <a href="purchase.html">Buy album</a>
        <span class="ui-li-count">12</span>
      </li>

      <li>
        <img src="rr_artwork.png" />
        <a href="radiohead_rainbows.html">In Rainbows</a>
        <a href="purchase.html">Buy album</a>
        <span class="ui-li-count">10</span>
      </li>

      <li>
        <img src="rk_artwork.png" />
        <a href="radiohead_kol.html">The King of Limbs</a>
        <a href="purchase.html">Buy album</a>
        <span class="ui-li-count">8</span>
      </li>
    </ul>
  </li>

  <!-- … -->
</ul>
```

The following screenshot shows the album cover next to the album name:

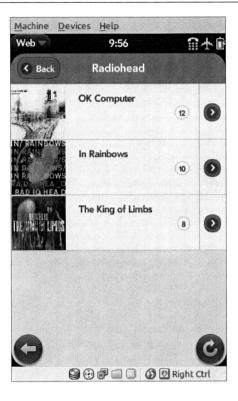

Alternatively, we can use regular 16 pixels square icons instead of an image: simply add the class `ul-li-icon` to the `img` tag.

Formatting content

Now that our list elements are bigger, we can add some more text, to give some more detailed information.

There are various ways in which we can modify the overall look of list items and content:

- Text hierarchy is added by using headers (increase emphasis) and paragraphs (reduce emphasis):

```
<ul data-role="listview">
  <!-- ... -->
  <li>Radiohead
    <ul data-list-icon="gear">
      <li>
        <img src="ro_artwork.png" />
```

```
          <a href="radiohead_ok.html">
            <h3>OK Computer</h3>
            <p>Capitol, 1995</p>
          </a>
          <a href="purchase.html">Buy album</a>
          <span class="ui-li-count">12</span>
        </li>

        <li>
          <img src="rr_artwork.png" />
          <a href="radiohead_rainbows.html">
            <h3>In Rainbows</h3>
            <p>Self-released, 2007</p>
          </a>
          <a href="purchase.html">Buy album</a>
          <span class="ui-li-count">10</span>
        </li>

        <li>
          <img src="rk_artwork.png" />
          <a href="radiohead_kol.html">
            <h3>The King of Limbs</h3>
            <p>Self-released, 2011</p>
          </a>
          <a href="purchase.html">Buy album</a>
          <span class="ui-li-count">8</span>
        </li>
      </ul>
    </li>

    <!-- … -->
  </ul>
```

A smaller line of text (label name) appears under the album name:

- Additional information can be added to the right of each list item by wrapping content in an element with a class of `ul-li-aside`.For example, here we are adding the track length (in minutes) to the right side of each list item in an album:

```
<!-- … -->
<li>Radiohead
  <ul>
    <!-- … -->
    <li>
      <img src="rk_artwork" />
      <h3><a href="#">The King of Limbs</a></h3>
      <p>Self-released, 2011</p>
        <ol>
          <li>
```

```
      <a href="#">Bloom</a>
      <p class="ui-li-aside">5:15</p>
    </li>
    <li>
      <a href="#">Morning Mr. Magpie</a>
      <p class="ui-li-aside">4:41</p>
    </li>
    <li>
      <a href="#">Little by Little</a>
      <p class="ui-li-aside">4:27</p>
    </li>
    <li>
      <a href="#">Feral</a>
      <p class="ui-li-aside">3:13</p>
    </li>
    <li>
      <a href="#">Lotus Flower</a>
      <p class="ui-li-aside">5:01</p>
    </li>
    <li>
      <a href="#">Codex</a>
      <p class="ui-li-aside">4:47</p>
    </li>
    <li>
      <a href="#">Give Up the Ghost</a>
      <p class="ui-li-aside">4:50</p>
    </li>
    <li>
      <a href="#">Separator</a>
      <p class="ui-li-aside">5:20</p>
    </li>
  </ol>
<a href="purchase.html">Buy album</a>
<span class="ui-li-count">8</span>
```

```
        </li>
      </ul>
    </li>
```

 Note that, in order to create a nested list with formatted content, we need to specify an anchor link for the text we wish to provide in the list item element. The link can also point to the same page (#), so we prevent jQuery Mobile from fetching another page and messing up coloring and the title/header of the nested list(s).

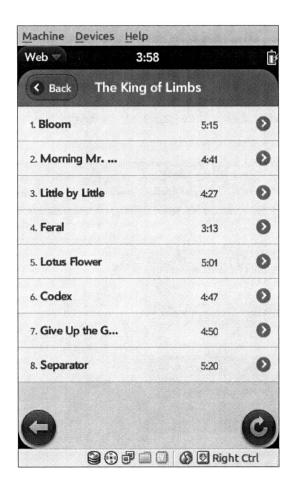

Implementing a search filter bar

As a last trick, in case we want to make it easier for the user to find their favorite artists, we may implement a search filter bar.

A search filter bar will look like an input element (search input) and will filter out all list elements that do not match with the user input in real time.

The search input will sit on top of the list and it can be included by adding a `data-filter="true"` attribute to the list:

```
<ul data-role="listview" data-filter="true">
  <li><a href="astra.html">Astra</a></li>
  <li><a href="zappa.html">Frank Zappa</a></li>
  <li><a href="tull.html">Jethro Tull</a></li>
  <li><a href="radiohead.html">Radiohead</a></li>
  <li><a href="who.html">The Who</a></li>
</ul>
```

The following screenshot shows how search filters work:

Summary

In this chapter, we have created a simple (not dynamic), jQuery Mobile-based music player interface, which has helped us in illustrating and understanding exactly what list views are and how we can use them in our own web applications.

API Calls and Properties

In this appendix, you can find a list of the API calls and properties to interact with jQuery Mobile internals.

List of properties and methods

The jQuery Mobile framework has some exposed variables and methods we can configure and use in our applications. Here is a list of them and their functioning. Please note we've already had a look at many of them in the preceding chapters, and these are reported here for easier reference only.

$.mobile options

The following options can be accessed using `$.mobile.[optionName]`:

Variable	Type	Default value
`activePageClass` (Class used for "active" button state, from CSS framework).	String	`ui-page-active`
`ajaxEnabled` (Automatically handle clicks and form submissions through Ajax, when the destination page is internal).	Boolean	`true`
`defaultTransition` (Set default page transition – dialog transition cannot be changed and is 'pop').	String	`slide`
`gradeA` (Support conditions that must be met in order to proceed – default is a function checking for media query support or IE 7+).	Function	

Variable	Type	Default value
`hashListeningEnabled` (Automatically load and show pages based on `location.hash`).	Boolean	`true`
`keyCode` (Assigns key codes. There is no reason to change this, but it may come in use in certain applications).	Object	
`loadingMessage` (Set the text that appears on page loading).	String	`loading`
`nonHistorySelectors` (Anchor links with a data-rel, or pages with a data-role, that match these selectors will be untrackable in history).	String	`dialog`
`normalizeRegex` (Compile the namespace normalization `regex` once).	string	`/-([a-z])/g`
`ns` (Namespace used framework-wide for data-attributes).	String	`""`
`pageLoadErrorMessage` (Error message that appears when an AJAX page request fails).	String	`Error Loading Page`
`subPageUrlKey` (Define the URL parameter used for referencing widget-generated sub-pages (that is, `example.html?ui-page=pageid`)).	String	`ui-page`

$.mobile methods

The following methods can be called with `$.mobile.[methodname]`:

- `addResolutionBreakPoints` (`int|array values`): Add width breakpoints to the min/max width classes that are added to the HTML element. Pass any number or array of numbers to add to the resolution classes.

- `base.reset` (`string href`): Set the generated BASE element's `href` attribute to a new page's base path.

- `base.set` (): Set the generated BASE element's `href` attribute to a new page's base path.

- `browser.ie` (): On-UA-based IE version check which allows for inclusion of IE 6+, including Windows Mobile 7.

- changePage (string|array|obj to[, string transition[, bool reverse=false[, bool changeHash=true]]]): Programmatically change from one page to another using a transition effect if specified or $.mobile. defaultTransition). Contrary to default behavior, you can specify a reverse transition (reverse=true) and make sure not to update hash to the page's URL when page change is complete (changeHash=false).

- The to argument is required and can be a string (URL), a jQuery object ($('#jqobj')), an object for sending form data, or an array specifying two page references ([from, to]) for transitioning from a known page (from) to a new one (to).

- nsNormalize (string prop): Takes a data attribute property (prop), prepends the namespace, then camel cases the attribute string.

- pageLoading ([bool Done=false]): Shows the page loading message if loading is not done.

- silentScroll ([int yPos=0]): Scrolls to a particular Y position without triggering scroll event listeners.

- url.getPrev (): Gets the previous page (in history) reference.

$.mobile.path methods

The following methods can be called using $.mobile.path.[methodName]:

- clean (string url): Returns a URL path with the window's location protocol/hostname/pathname removed.

- getFilePath (string path): Returns the substring of a filepath before the sub-page key, for making a server request.

- hasProtocol (string url): Checks whether a URL has a different protocol (that is, ftp, mailto).

- isExternal (string url): Checks whether a URL is external or under the same domain.

- isEmbeddedPage (string url): Checks whether a URL refers to a page already in the DOM.

- isRelative (string url): Checks whether a URL is relative.

- makeAbsolute (string url): Prefixes a relative URL with the current path.

- setOrigin (): Sets the path.origin property to the currently viewed URL path.

- stripHash (string url): Returns the URL without an initial '#'.

$.mobile.path properties

The following property can be accessed using `$.mobile.path.[propertyName]`:

Property	Type
`origin` (location pathname from initial directory request.)	`string`

$.mobile.urlHistory methods

The following methods can be called using `$.mobile.urlHistory.[methodName]`:

- `clearForward ()`: Wipes URLs ahead of active index.
- `GetActive ()`: Gets the active page reference (not URL!).
- `getNext ()`: Gets the next page (in history) reference – if any.

$.mobile.urlHistory properties

The following properties can be accessed using `$.mobile.urlHistory.[propertyname]`:

Property	Type
`activeIndex` (Index of the active page in the stack)	`int`
`stack` (array of pages that are visited during a single page load. Each has a URL and optional transition)	`array`

$.support tests

A handful of properties and methods are available to use for testing whether the mobile browser/platform supports features jQuery Mobile makes use of. The following properties return either true or false if the corresponding feature is (respectively) supported or not:

- `$.support.boxShadow`
- `$.support.cssPseudoElement`
- `$.support.cssTransitions`
- `$.support.dynamicBaseTag`
- `$.support.eventCapture`
- `$.support.mediaquery`
- `$.support.orientation`
- `$.support.pushState`

- `$.support.scrollTop`
- `$.support.touch`

Button plugin

Button elements are covered in *Chapters 6, Mobile Clicking: Buttons* and *Chapter 7, Mobile Clicking: Buttons.*

The following options can be modified to match your own liking from the `mobileinit` event: `$.mobile.button.prototype.options.[optionName]:`

Option	Type	Default value
corners	Bool	true
icon	String	Null
iconpos	String (i.e. topleft)	Null
iconshadow	Bool	true
inline	Bool	Null
shadow	Bool	true
theme	String (i.e. 'a', 'b')	null

To disable a `#button` element: `$('#button').button ('disable').`

To enable a `#button` element: `$('#button').button ('enable').`

Check and radio boxes plugin

Checkboxes and radio buttons are covered in *Chapter 7, Mobile Clicking: Buttons.*

The following option can be modified to match your own liking from the `mobileinit` event: `$.mobile.checkboxradio.prototype.options.[optionName]:`

Option	Type	Default value
theme	String (i.e. 'a', 'b')	null

To disable a `#radio` element: `$('#radio').checkboxradio ('disable')` to enable a `#radio` element: `$('#radio').checkboxradio ('enable').`

If you make any changes to this kind of elements and/or their labels, you may want to refresh in order to update changes with `$('#radio').checkboxradio ('refresh');`

Collapsible plugin

Collapsible blocks are covered in *Chapter 4*.

The following options can be modified to match your own liking from the `mobileinit` event: `$.mobile.collapsible.prototype.options.[optionName]`.

Option	Type	Default value
expandCueText	String	' click to expand contents'
collapseCueText	String	' click to collapse contents'
collapsed	Bool	false
heading	String	'>:header,>legend'
iconTheme	String	'd'
theme	String (i.e. 'a', 'b')	null

Dialog plugin

Dialogs are covered in *Chapter 2, Organizing Content: Pages and Dialogs*.

To close a `#dialog` element: `$('#dialog').dialog ('close')`.

If you don't know the ID of the dialog you want to close, you can close it with `$('.ui-dialog').dialog('close')`.

List view plugin

List views are covered in *Chapter 8, Organizing Information: List Views*.

The following options can be modified to match your own liking from the `mobileinit` event: `$.mobile.listview.prototype.options.[optionName]`:

Option	Type	Default value
countTheme	String (i.e. 'a', 'b')	'c'
dividerTheme	String (i.e. 'a', 'b')	'b'
headerTheme	String (i.e. 'a', 'b')	'b'
inset	Bool	false
splitIcon	String (i.e. 'a', 'b')	'arrow-r'
splitTheme	String (i.e. 'a', 'b')	'b'
theme	String (i.e. 'a', 'b')	'c'

We can access the refresh method with `$('#listview').listview ('refresh')`.

Navbar plugin

Navigation bars are covered in *Chapter 2, Organizing Content: Pages and Dialogs*.

The following options can be modified to match your own liking from the `mobileinit` event: `$.mobile.navbar.prototype.options.[optionName]`:

Option	Type	Default value
iconpos	String (i.e. 'left')	'top'
grid	Bool	null

Page plugin

Pages are covered in *Chapter 2, Organizing Content: Pages and Dialogs*.

The following options can be modified to match your own liking from the `mobileinit` event: `$.mobile.page.prototype.options.[optionName]`:

Option	Type	Default value
addBackBtn	Bool	true
backBtnText	String	'Back'
degradeInputs	Object	
keepNative	Bool	null

In the `degradeInput` object, we can choose whether we want the following elements to be degraded or not (they are all default to false, and range to "number"): `color`, `date`, `datetime`, `datetime-local`, `email`, `month`, `number`, `range`, `search`, `tel`, `time`, `url`, `week`.

Select plugin

Select menus are covered in *Chapter 7, Mobile Clicking: Buttons*.

The following options can be modified to match your own liking from the `mobileinit` event: `$.mobile.select.prototype.options.[optionName]`:

Option	Type	Default value
corners	Bool	true
closeText	String	'Close'

Option	Type	Default value
disabled	Bool	false
hidePlaceHolderMenuItems	Bool	true
icon	String	'arrow-d'
iconpos	String (i.e. left)	'right'
iconshadow	Bool	true
inline	Bool	null
menuPageTheme	String	'b'
nativeMenu	Bool	false
overlayTheme	String	'a'
shadow	Bool	true
theme	String (i.e. 'a', 'b')	null

You can programmatically open and close the menu of a #select element with `$('#select').select ('open')` and `$('#select').select ('close')`.

Selects can be enabled/disabled using `$('#select').select ('enable')`/`$('#select').select ('disable')`.

To update changes, use `$('#select').select ('refresh')`.

Slider plugin

Slider elements are covered in *Chapter 7, Mobile Clicking: Buttons*.

The following options can be modified to match your own liking from the `mobileinit` event: `$.mobile.slider.prototype.options.[optionName]`.

Option	Type	Default value
disabled	Bool	false
theme	String (i.e. 'a', 'b')	null
trackTheme	Bool	null

Sliders can be enabled ('enable'), disabled ('disable'), and updated ('refresh'): `$('#slider').slider ('disable');`

Text input plugin

Text inputs are covered in *Chapter 7, Mobile Clicking: Buttons*.

The following options can be modified to match your own liking from the `mobileinit` event: `$.mobile.textinput.prototype.options.[optionName]`:

Option	Type	Default value
theme	String (i.e. 'a', 'b')	null

Input elements (#text) can be enabled and disabled using the textinput plugin: $('#text').textinput ('enable').

JqmData: Whenever we need to check, or programmatically set or remove, a data attribute, we need to make use of the mobile-friendly versions of the data methods.

- $.jqmData
- $.jqmHasData
- $.jqmRemoveData

These can be called either as a standalone function: $.jqmRemoveData (element, property) or directly on an element: $('#element').jqmRemoveData (property).

Please note these functions take care of adding the (eventual) namespace (ns) to the data attribute, so if our namespace is myns- and we need to modify a mydata data, the core $.data function will be passed the value myns-mydata.

data-* attributes: The following data attributes can be specified in the markup:

Attribute	Value(s)	Notes	Element(s)
data-role	button	Button element	
	collapsible	Collapsible element	
	content	Sub page element	
	controlgroup	Radio, checkbox or button parent element	
	fieldcontain	Fieldset element	
	footer	Sub page element	
	header	Sub page element	
	list-divider	Sub Listview element	
	listview	Listview element	
	navbar	Navigation bar element	
	page	Page element	
	slider	Slider element	
	none	Leave element untouched by jQuery Mobile	
data-theme	a, b, c, d, e	Set theme	All
data-icon	See icon list below	Set button icon	Buttons

Attribute	Value(s)	Notes	Element(s)
data-iconpos	bottom left (default) top right	Place the icon accordingly	Elements with an icon
	notext	Remove text (icon only)	
data-collapsed	true	Collapsed by default	Collapsible block
data-type	horizontal	Show options horizontally	Control group
data-position	fixed	Stay at top/bottom	Headers
	inline	Normal HTML behavior (default)	Footers
	fullscreen	Only visible on screen tap	
data-ajax	false	Same as rel=external	Links
data-direction	reverse	Reverse transition (without going back in history)	Links
data-rel	back	Mimic back button behavior	Links
	dialog	Open link as a dialog	
data-transition	fade flip pop slide slideup slidedown	Transition effect	Links
data-dividertheme	a, b, c, d, e	Set divider theme	List dividers
data-filter	true	Make a list filterable	Listviews
data-filter-placeholder	Default: "Filter items..."	Set input's placeholder text	Listviews
data-inset	true	Apply inset appearance to a listview	Listviews
data-split-icon	See icon list below	Set split icon	Listviews
data-split-theme	a, b, c, d, e	Set split theme	Listviews

Attribute	Value(s)	Notes	Element(s)
data-placeholder	true	Option which serves as a placeholder in a select menu	Menu element
data-add-back-btn	true	Show back button (disabled by default)	Nav bars
data-back-btn-text	Default: "Back"	Configure back button text	Nav bars
data-url	Page location identifier		Pages
data-native-menu	false	Use custom menu on a specific select element	Select menus

Icons: The data-icon attribute accepts the following icons (apart from the custom ones):

Icon name	Icon
alert	⚠
arrow-d	⌄
arrow-l	❮
arrow-r	❯
arrow-u	⌃
back	↺
check	✔
delete	✖
forward	↻
gear	⚙
grid	⦂⦂⦂
home	⌂

Icon name	Icon
info	i
minus	▬
plus	✚
refresh	↻
search	🔍
star	★

B
Resources and Troubleshooting

In this appendix, you can find a list of useful resources, development tools, and troubleshooting in order to better understand how jQuery (Mobile) and JavaScript work together.

Online and offline resources

If this topic is of any interest to you, you may be wondering how to learn more. Books and (mainly) online documentation can help a great deal in getting a better grasp of JavaScript, jQuery, and jQuery Mobile.

Official jQuery and jQuery Mobile documentation

Here are some official websites where you can find a lot of useful information, featuring examples and user comments:

- `http://docs.jquery.com`
- `http://jquerymobile.com/demos/`

jQuery 1.4 reference guide

Written by Jonathan Chaffer and Karl Swedberg, it is "a comprehensive exploration of the popular JavaScript library".

`https://www.packtpub.com/jquery-1-4-reference-guide/book`

jQuery mobile gallery

JQM Gallery (by Dan Tavelli) was started to showcase jQuery mobile sites/apps and be a place to go for inspiration and ideas for your next project.

It also features a handful of tutorials and books dealing with jQuery Mobile.

`http://www.jqmgallery.com`.

Development tools

Utilities and development tools are essential for the savvy developer. Here are some you may find useful.

FireBug (Firefox)

Essential for the jQuery developer, Firebug integrates with Firefox to put a wealth of web development tools at your fingertips while you browse. You can edit, debug, and monitor CSS, HTML, and JavaScript live in any web page.

Get it from `http://getfirebug.com`.

Also, the possibility to write Firebug's own extensions has contributed to the creation of FireQuery (`http://firequery.binaryage.com`), a Firebug extension for jQuery development.

Internet Explorer 8 developer tools

Microsoft published a guide on using Internet Explorer 8 built in Developer Tools suite at `http://msdn.microsoft.com/en-us/library/dd565622%28v=VS.85%29.aspx`, which also explains how to debug JavaScript code with their debugging tool.

Safari web inspector

Safari comes with a built-in web inspector tool to analyze DOM and JavaScript.

To enable the Web Inspector, open the `Preferences` and check the **Show develop menu in the menu bar** item in the **Advanced Preferences** pane.

Web Inspector: `http://trac.webkit.org/wiki/WebInspector`.

Dragonfly (Opera)

The built-in tool is very promising and allows for CSS, DOM inspection and editing, and JavaScript debugging.

You can read more about this tool at `http://www.opera.com/dragonfly/`.

Chrome web inspector

The web inspector is enabled by default, and can be accessed using the **Inspect Element** context menu.

More information available at `http://www.google.com/chrome/intl/en/webmasters-faq.html#tools`.

Web Inspector: `http://trac.webkit.org/wiki/WebInspector`.

Troubleshooting

Sometimes we face common problems we need to get sorted out right away.
Here is a list with issues and questions you may encounter and how to solve them.

Mobile equivalent of $(document).ready

If we're used to working with jQuery, we may get a bit confused on how we can fire our function after the DOM is ready.

To trigger a similar document-ready event on pages loaded with AJAX, we can put the code we need to be executed inside a `pageshow` event: the function (or code) will then be executed each time the page is shown.

You may want to check out the `pagecreate` event to make sure your code is executed at the exact moment you want it to.

Target object

Consider the following code:

```
$('#element').bind ('swipe', function (e) {
    var targetElement = e.target;
});
```

To get the target element (the one we swiped on) we use `e.target`.

Creating custom themes and swatches

The jQuery Mobile framework makes it easy to create, add new themes, and modify existing ones through a theming system which is very simple to understand.

Before we begin, we must have a really clear idea what is, essentially, a jQuery Mobile swatch: each time we specify a data-theme attribute, the framework selects the color swatch we have specified from the CSS files of them we are using.

The separation of a theme (in which are defined structural styles) and swatches (colors and texture) is essential to achieve a wide range of visual effects.

New themes are composed of a stylesheet in which a number of color swatches are defined. Obviously, the theme can include images, changes in borders, padding, margins, and so on: it's all up to you.

To use a theme you have created, you need to add a link to the CSS right before the `</head>` tag:

```
<link rel="stylesheet" href="mynewtheme.css" />
```

As for swatches, jQuery Mobile dynamically looks for a CSS class that matches the swatch you have specified. So, for example, a `data-theme="c"` attribute added to a button will make jQuery Mobile apply the `ui-btn-hover-c` class anytime we hover the button, whereas `data-theme="b"` applies the `ui-btn-hover-b` class.

To create a new swatch for an existing theme, we basically copy the whole block of code for one swatch (that is, "a") and rename all selectors appropriately (that is, `ui-btn-hover-a` becomes `.ui-btn-hover-g`, and so on).

You can choose any letter but a, b, c, d, and e, as they are already used by jQuery Mobile.

After we have tweaked our G swatch, we can add a `data-theme="g"` attribute to our elements and see our custom swatch in action.

Index

Symbols

appearance 124, 126

H

hashListeningEnabled option 53, 176
hasProtocol method 177
header bar, jQuery Mobile
  about 89
  buttons, customizing 90-94
  creating 89, 90
headerTheme option 180
heading option 180
hidePlaceHolderMenuItems option 182
history, jQuery Mobile 8
history, Sencha Touch 11
home icon 185
HP WebOS 7
href attribute 92
HTML5 standard 25

I

icon option 179, 182
iconpos option 179-182
icons
  about 117
  buttons, creating with 117-120
icons, data-icon attribute
  alert 185
  arrow-d 185
  arrow-l 185
  arrow-r 185
  arrow-u 185
  back 185
  check 185
  delete 185
  forward 185
  gear 185
  grid 185
  home 185
  info 186
  minus 186
  plus 186
  refresh 186
  search 186
  star 186
iconshadow option 179, 182
iconTheme option 180

id attribute 30
images
  adding, to list item 165, 167
img tag 165
index.html file 30
info icon 186
inline buttons 121-124
inline option 179, 182
input elements, jQuery Mobile framework
  about 131
  search inputs 135
  text inputs 132-135
inset option 180
internal links 35
internal pages
  about 34
  linking, with external pages 35
  versus external pages 34
Internet Explorer 8 developer tools 188
iOS 7
iPhone application 10
iphonenav 13
isEmbeddedPage method 177
isExternal method 177
isRelative method 177
iUI
  about 13
  features 14
  users 13
iWebKit
  about 14
  display 15
  features 15
  users 15

J

JavaScript API 11
JQM Gallery
  about 188
  URL 188
jQTouch
  display 10
  features 11
  users 9, 10
  versus jQuery Mobile 9
  website link 10

Thank you for buying
jQuery Mobile First Look

About Packt Publishing

Packt, pronounced 'packed', published its first book "*Mastering phpMyAdmin for Effective MySQL Management*" in April 2004 and subsequently continued to specialize in publishing highly focused books on specific technologies and solutions.

Our books and publications share the experiences of your fellow IT professionals in adapting and customizing today's systems, applications, and frameworks. Our solution based books give you the knowledge and power to customize the software and technologies you're using to get the job done. Packt books are more specific and less general than the IT books you have seen in the past. Our unique business model allows us to bring you more focused information, giving you more of what you need to know, and less of what you don't.

Packt is a modern, yet unique publishing company, which focuses on producing quality, cutting-edge books for communities of developers, administrators, and newbies alike. For more information, please visit our website: www.packtpub.com.

About Packt Open Source

In 2010, Packt launched two new brands, Packt Open Source and Packt Enterprise, in order to continue its focus on specialization. This book is part of the Packt Open Source brand, home to books published on software built around Open Source licences, and offering information to anybody from advanced developers to budding web designers. The Open Source brand also runs Packt's Open Source Royalty Scheme, by which Packt gives a royalty to each Open Source project about whose software a book is sold.

Writing for Packt

We welcome all inquiries from people who are interested in authoring. Book proposals should be sent to author@packtpub.com. If your book idea is still at an early stage and you would like to discuss it first before writing a formal book proposal, contact us; one of our commissioning editors will get in touch with you.

We're not just looking for published authors; if you have strong technical skills but no writing experience, our experienced editors can help you develop a writing career, or simply get some additional reward for your expertise.

jQuery 1.4 Reference Guide

ISBN: 9781849510042   Paperback: 336pages

A comprehensive exploration of the popular JavaScript library

1. Quickly look up features of the jQuery library

2. Step through each function, method, and selector expression in the jQuery library with an easy-to-follow approach

3. Understand the anatomy of a jQuery script

4. Write your own plug-ins using jQuery's powerful plug-in architecture

jQuery 1.4 Animation Techniques: Beginners Guide

ISBN: 978-1-84951-330-2   Paperback: 344 pages

Quickly master all of jQuery's animation methods and build a toolkit of ready-to-use animations using jQuery 1.4

1. Create both simple and complex animations using clear, step-by-step instructions, accompanied with screenshots

2. Walk through each of jQuery's built-in animation methods and see in detail how each one can be used

3. Over 50 detailed examples of different types of web page animations

Please check **www.PacktPub.com** for information on our titles

jQuery Plugin Development Beginner's Guide

ISBN: 978-1-849512-24-4   Paperback: 288 pages

Build powerful, interactive plugins to implement jQuery in the best way possible

1. Utilize jQuery's plugin framework to create a wide range of useful jQuery plugins from scratch

2. Understand development patterns and best practices and move up the ladder to master plugin development

3. Discover the ins and outs of some of the most popular jQuery plugins in action

PHP jQuery Cookbook

ISBN: 978-1-84951-274-9   Paperback: 332 pages

Over 60 simple but highly effective recipes to create interactive web applications using PHP with jQuery

1. Create rich and interactive web applications with PHP and jQuery

2. Debug and execute jQuery code on a live site

3. Another title in the Packt Cookbook range, which will help you get to grips with PHP as well as jQuery

Please check **www.PacktPub.com** for information on our titles

CMS Design Using PHP and jQuery

ISBN: 978-1-84951-252-7   Paperback: 340 pages

Build and improve your in-house PHP CMS by enhancing it with jQuery

1. Create a completely functional and a professional looking CMS

2. Add a modular architecture to your CMS and create template-driven web designs

3. Use jQuery plugins to enhance the "feel" of your CMS

Joomla! 1.5 JavaScript jQuery

ISBN: 978-1-849512-04-6   Paperback: 292 pages

Enhance your Joomla! Sites with the power of jQuery extensions, plugins, and more

1. Build impressive Joomla! Sites with JavaScript and jQuery

2. Create your own Joomla!, jQuery-powered, extensions

3. Enhance your site with third-party features, code-highlighting, Flicker, and more using Joomla! Plugins

Please check **www.PacktPub.com** for information on our titles

Lightning Source UK Ltd.
Milton Keynes UK
UKOW011952221111

182498UK00004B/5/P